Wyoming

Wyoming

Deborah Kent

Children's Press®
A Division of Grolier Publishing
New York   London   Hong Kong   Sydney
Danbury, Connecticut

Frontispiece: Grand Teton National Park

Front cover: Yellowstone National Park Lower Falls

Back cover: Devils Tower National Monument

Consultant: Priscilla Golden, Wyoming State Library

Please note: All statistics are as up-to-date as possible at the time of publication.

Visit Children's Press on the Internet at http://publishing.grolier.com

Book production by Editorial Directions, Inc.

Library of Congress Cataloging-in-Publication Data

Kent, Deborah.
   Wyoming / by Deborah Kent.
      144 p. 24 cm. — (America the beautiful. Second series)
   Includes bibliographical references (p. 136) and index.
   Summary : Describes the geography, plants, animals, history, economy, language,
     religions, culture, sports, art, and people of the state of Wyoming.
   ISBN 0-516-21075-0
   1. Wyoming—Juvenile literature. [1. Wyoming.] I. Title. II. Series.
F761.3.K46 2000
978.7—dc21
                                                           99-36348
                                                             CIP
                                                             AC

GROLIER
PUBLISHING

Acknowledgments

I would like to thank the curators at the Wyoming State Museum in Cheyenne for their suggestions and guidance during the preparation of this book. I also wish to express my appreciation to the staff of the Wyoming State Library in Cheyenne for helping me uncover valuable resources. As always, special thanks go to my reader and research assistant, Natalie Ludena, for her thoroughness, perseverance, and commitment throughout this project.

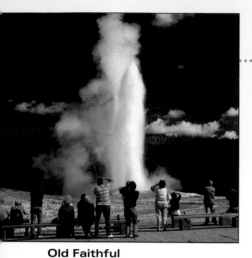

Old Faithful

Mount Moran

Lower Yellowstone Falls

Contents

Western meadowlark

Wyoming cowboy

Vacationers canoeing

Wyoming youth

Bison

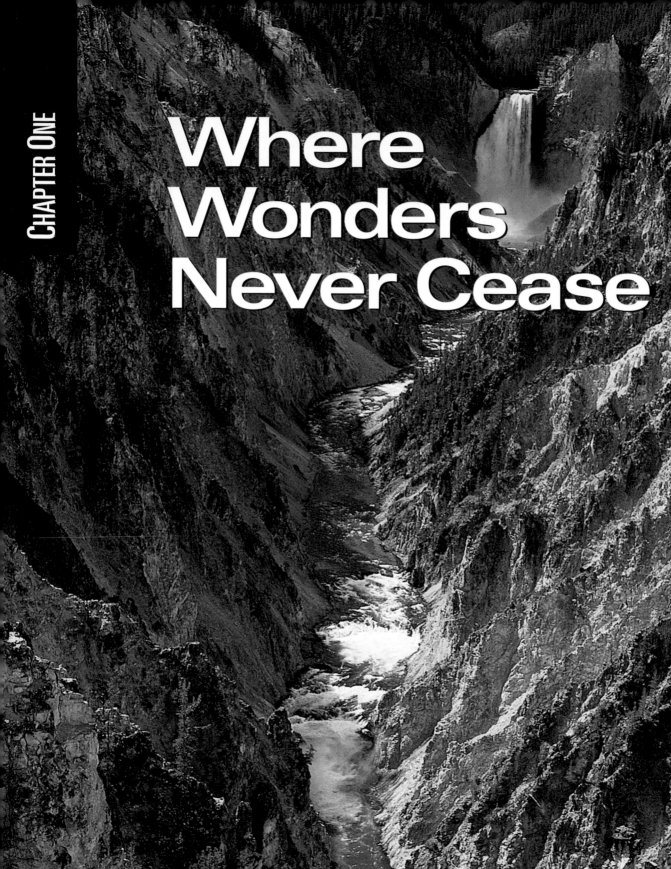

CHAPTER ONE

Where Wonders Never Cease

A crowd watching
Old Faithful geyser
at Yellowstone
National Park

Throughout the day, crowds gather at Old Faithful geyser in Wyoming's Yellowstone National Park. Cameras ready, the spectators wait for the show to begin. Every 20 to 120 minutes, a low rumble comes from somewhere deep within the Earth. A plume of steam hisses up from the geyser's crater. The plume grows and rises, and the hiss swells to a roar. As the spellbound crowd watches, a column of boiling water shoots to the height of a twelve-story building. A hundred dazzling rainbows dance and caper in the sunlight. The breeze catches wisps of vapor and sends them streaming toward the mountains. Then, slowly at first, the tower starts to collapse. The roar fades and the column of water and steam sinks away. Nothing remains but a silent crater in the ground.

Old Faithful is the most famous attraction in Yellowstone. The park sprawls across 2.2 million acres (891,000 hectares) of northwestern Wyoming, spilling across the borders into Montana and Idaho. It embraces majestic mountains, thundering waterfalls, and

Opposite: Yellowstone
River canyon

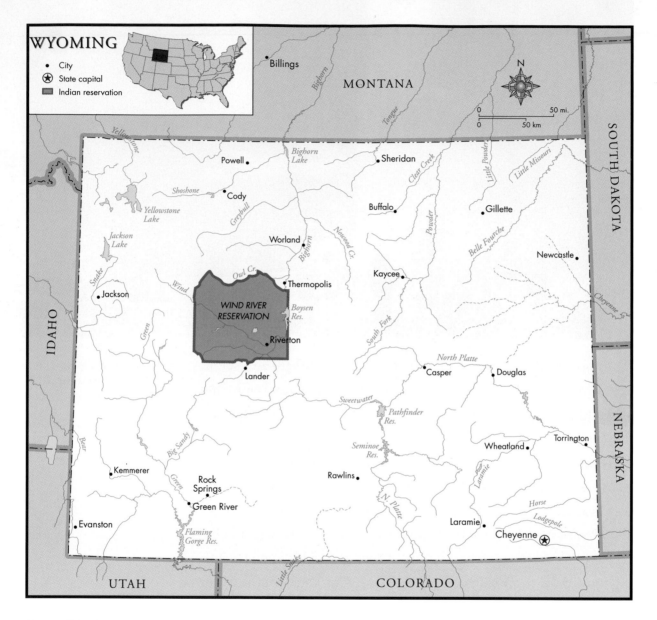

WYOMING

- • City
- ⭐ State capital
- ▪ Indian reservation

MONTANA

SOUTH DAKOTA

IDAHO

NEBRASKA

Billings

Powell

Cody

Yellowstone Lake

Jackson Lake

Jackson

Sheridan

Buffalo

Gillette

Newcastle

Worland

Thermopolis

Kaycee

WIND RIVER RESERVATION

Boysen Res.

Riverton

Lander

Casper

Douglas

Wheatland

Torrington

Kemmerer

Rock Springs

Green River

Rawlins

Laramie

Cheyenne ⭐

Evanston

UTAH

COLORADO

N

0   50 mi.

0   50 km

**Geopolitical map of
Wyoming**

deep, clear lakes. There are plunging canyons and high meadows
bright with wildflowers. Thousands of elk live in the park, as well
as mule deer, black bears, bison, and even a few giant grizzlies.

Yellowstone is the oldest national park in the world. It was
established in 1872, when the United States was less than a century

old. Already the young nation was filling up with people. Settlers from the eastern states pressed farther and farther westward. A widening band of settlements stretched up and down the Pacific Coast too. One last region of the country remained relatively untouched —the rugged expanse of the northern Rocky Mountains, including present-day Wyoming. The land there was too harsh to produce abundant crops, and it held no great stores of gold or silver. To most Americans, Wyoming Territory was a useless wasteland.

Yellowstone is home to bison and other wildlife.

Yet Wyoming surpassed other regions with the variety and beauty of its natural wonders. Congress recognized that some of its unique landscape should be protected to enrich future generations. Today 2.6 million acres (1 million ha) of land in Wyoming is devoted to parks and wildlife preserves. Wyoming's scenic wonders attract millions of visitors each year.

Wyoming is still sparsely populated compared to other states in the Union. Its cities are few and widely scattered. Most Wyomingites prefer it that way. They love their uncluttered vistas and long, empty stretches of road. They enjoy working and playing in the great outdoors. Wyoming may not have the variety of stores and movie theaters available in more urbanized states, but neither does it have urban crime and traffic jams. One popular slogan claims, "Wyoming is what America was."

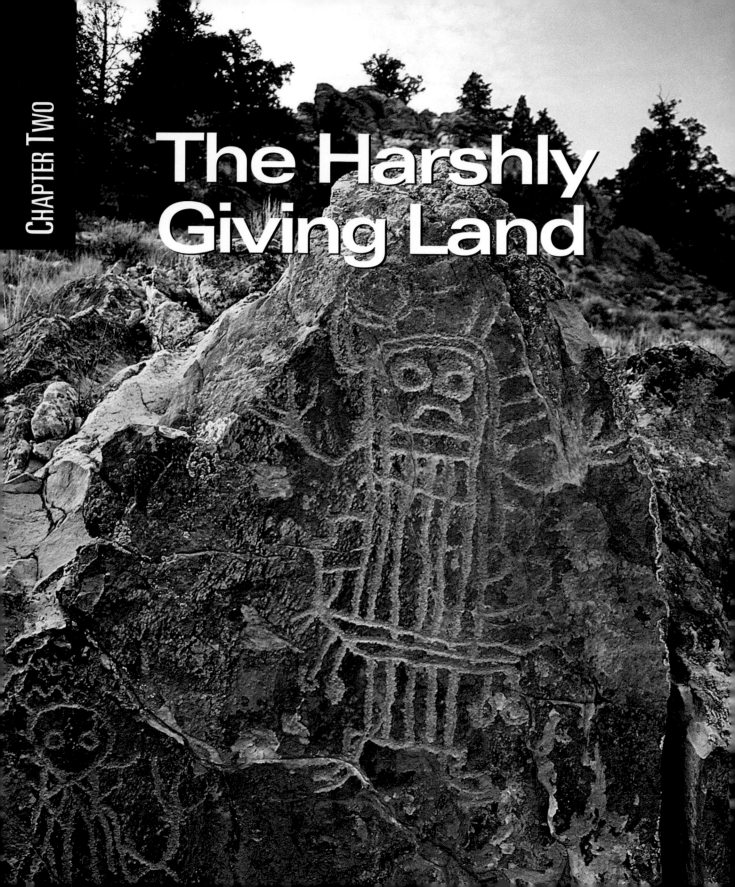

Chapter Two

The Harshly Giving Land

In the Bighorn Mountains west of Sheridan, Wyoming, stands a mysterious circle of stones known as the Medicine Wheel. The circle measures 243 feet (74 meters) in diameter. At its center is a cairn—a pile of stones—about 3 feet (1 m) high. Some archaeologists believe that this cairn represents the sun. Twenty-eight lines of stones radiate from the cairn like the spokes of a wheel. They probably represent the days in each cycle of the moon as it waxes and wanes. The Medicine Wheel was doubtless used in some form of ancient ritual. But how it was used and who built it are unsolved mysteries. When the Europeans asked the Native Americans in the late 1800s, they were told that the circle was made long ago "by the people who had no iron."

The Medicine Wheel was perhaps used as part of an ancient ritual.

Opposite: Petroglyphs at Wind River Reservation

The People Who Had No Iron

The first humans to live in Wyoming were probably the descendants of Asian nomads. They followed the animals they hunted across a land bridge that then existed between Siberia and present-day Alaska. In Wyoming, stone spearpoints have been found among the bones of mammoths and bison, remains that date to about 9000 B.C. Those early people carved axes, spearpoints, arrowheads, knives, and scrapers from quartzite, chalcedony, and other kinds of stone. These minerals were preferred because they could be chipped away easily, leaving a strong, sharp edge.

Archaeologists sometimes find piles of bones at the foot of a cliff or in the bottom of a steep gully. These discoveries suggest that the hunters pursued their game and drove the animals over cliffs. Sometimes they chased the animals into deep sand that prevented them from running away. Once trapped, even a large creature such as a mammoth could be killed with a well-aimed spear.

An archaeological site in Lincoln County

Much of the stone used by these early people came from quarries near what is now the town of Lusk. For 40 miles (64 kilometers) the land is dotted with holes about 20 feet (6 m) across and 15 to 20 feet (4.6 to 6 m) deep. Around each hole are heaps of earth and broken rock, debris the miners left behind. As the ancient people had no metal, all the quarrying was done with stone tools. They pounded a stone wedge into a rock seam with a stone hammer. Eventually, with tremendous effort, the rock was cracked apart to reveal the sought-after minerals within. Archaeologists who study these Wyoming quarries have found some stone wedges jammed into place, just waiting for hammer blows to drive them deeper.

Around 7000 B.C., the climate in Wyoming began to change. Grasslands dried up as rainfall decreased, and the herds of game moved away. Most of Wyoming's human inhabitants followed the deer and bison. For the next 2,000 years, Wyoming had very few people. Humans began to return around 4500 B.C., most likely

The Spanish Diggings

Wandering cowboys discovered Wyoming's ancient quartzite quarries in the 1870s. The cowboys believed that the mines were the legacy of Spanish explorers searching for gold. They never imagined that Native Americans might have dug the mines. In the 1890s, scientists from several East Coast museums and universities visited Wyoming to study the mines. They concluded that it was not Spaniards but prehistoric North American peoples who made the strange pits. Nevertheless, the quarries are still known to Wyomingites as the Spanish Diggings. ∎

Wyoming's early residents followed and hunted herds of bison.

Pictures on Stone

Traces of ancient inhabitants are still seen on some of Wyoming's cliffs and canyon walls. The region's early inhabitants carved pictures into stone or painted images with dyes made from plants. The carvings are called petroglyphs, and the paintings are known as pictographs. No one knows how the work was done, but it shows us the resourcefulness of Wyoming's first people. Did the artists stand on ladders as they worked? Or did they lower themselves down the sheer rock by ropes anchored at the top? We can only guess as we gaze at their creations in wonder. ■

due to a more favorable climate shift, but they never came in great numbers. The soil was poor, the terrain was rugged, and winters were brutally cold. While vast herds of bison flourished on the Great Plains to the east, the sparse vegetation of Wyoming's canyons and mountainsides could not feed large numbers of game. Wyoming was an uninviting place, and most hunters left it alone.

Thundering Hoofbeats

Sometime during the 1700s, small bands of hunters began moving into the Wyoming region from the west. These were the tribes known today as the Crow and Shoshone Indians. Within a few generations two more groups, the Arapaho and the Cheyenne, entered the region from the northeast. Then, early in the nineteenth century, the Sioux pushed westward into Wyoming. Other tribes also migrated into the region—the Nez Perce, the Gros Ventre, the Bannock, the Kiowa, and the Flathead. (The Flathead got their name from their custom of fastening a board across an infant's fore-

A settlement of the
Gros Ventre tribe

head, causing the face to develop a flattened appearance.) All of these groups were relatively small. Counted together, they probably numbered not more than 10,000 people in the region that is Wyoming today.

These migrations into Wyoming reflected dramatic changes in the entire area west of the Mississippi. In 1610, Spanish colonists had established a mission at Santa Fe, New Mexico. With the coming of the Spaniards, the Indians encountered horses for the first time. They were eager to own these extraordinary beasts that could gallop so fast and carry riders and supplies on their backs. The Indians traded for horses, stole horses, and captured horses that had wandered into the mountains and gone wild. Some historians believe that the Eastern Shoshone were accomplished horse traders as early as 1700.

The coming of the horse transformed life for the Indians of the Great Plains. Horses were a tremendous asset in hunting and warfare. Tribes such as the Sioux and Cheyenne gained great military

Native Americans gained military strength when they began using horses.

power. They expanded their territory, driving weaker groups away from the best hunting grounds. The result was a vast reshuffling of peoples on the plains and in the northern Rocky Mountains. Forced from their traditional lands by constant warfare, tribes moved into the largely unoccupied land of Wyoming.

For the most part, the Indians of Wyoming were nomadic people. They moved with the seasons and did not build permanent towns. Their food came from hunting and gathering wild fruits and vegetables. Each Native American group had its own distinct language and customs. The Shoshone lived chiefly in the mountainous western half of the state. The Crow lived in the Bighorn Mountains in the north. The eastern plains were the home of the Cheyenne, Arapaho, and Sioux.

Bird Woman on the Trail

When she was twelve years old, a Shoshone girl named Sacajawea (1787?–1812) was captured by a neighboring tribe. She was sold as a slave to the Mandan Indians in present-day North Dakota. Eventually Sacajawea, also known as Bird Woman, married a French-Canadian trader named Toussaint Charbonneau. Charbonneau joined the exploring expedition of Meriwether Lewis and William Clark in 1805. Sacajawea and her infant son also accompanied the expedition on its long journey to the Pacific coast. The young Shoshone woman was an invaluable guide and interpreter. She also helped to keep the peace when the expedition encountered bands of Indians. At one point, by an amazing coincidence, they even met her brother, whom she had not seen in fourteen years. After the expedition, Sacajawea returned to her own people. She died in what is now the Wind River Reservation in Wyoming. ■

The Eastern, or Wind River, Shoshone were not organized into a single tribe led by a strong chief. Instead they lived in small nomadic bands in which most members were related. Once or twice a year, several of these bands gathered to hunt or dance. The Shoshone made shelters of branches and grasses or built tepees of animal skins.

In Search of the Beaver

The first Europeans to enter Wyoming were two brothers from French Canada, François and Louis-Joseph La Vérendrye. In 1742, the La Vérendrye brothers set out from present-day Manitoba to search for a route to the Pacific Ocean. Their journey carried them to Wyoming's northeastern corner, but they never reached their destination. Though the La Vérendryes turned back, other French

Fur trappers often traded with Native Americans.

explorers made forays into Wyoming over the years that followed. Most trapped beaver, fox, and other fur-bearing animals or traded for furs with the Indians. The French and the Indians got along fairly well. The trappers learned Indian languages and sometimes married Indian women. But they were still outsiders, and their presence disturbed the Indians' way of life. One trapper wrote in a letter to a Canadian fur company that the Indians "seemed to desire that I go away."

In 1803, the newly formed United States bought a vast tract of land from France. This land deal, called the Louisiana Purchase, more than doubled the country's size. President Thomas Jefferson sent an expedition under Meriwether Lewis and William Clark to explore this immense new territory. The expedition traveled from present-day Missouri all the way to the mouth of the Columbia River in Oregon.

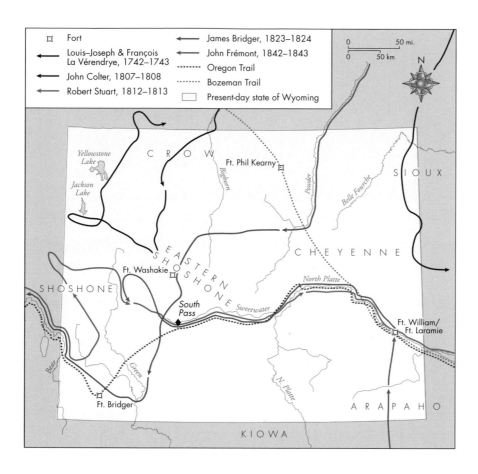

Fort

Louis–Joseph & François La Vérendrye, 1742–1743

John Colter, 1807–1808

Robert Stuart, 1812–1813

James Bridger, 1823–1824

John Frémont, 1842–1843

Oregon Trail

Bozeman Trail

Present-day state of Wyoming

0   50 mi.
0   50 km

N

C R O W

Yellowstone Lake

Jackson Lake

Ft. Phil Kearny

SIOUX

Bighorn

Powder

Belle Fourche

E A S T E R N S H O S H O N E

Ft. Washakie

C H E Y E N N E

North Platte

SHOSHONE

South Pass

Sweetwater

Ft. William/ Ft. Laramie

Green

N. Platte

Bear

Ft. Bridger

A R A P A H O

K I O W A

Exploration of Wyoming

The Lewis and Clark expedition did not enter Wyoming. But as the group headed home, one of its members, Captain John Colter, left to explore on his own. For the next four years, Colter traveled the rivers of the northern Rockies, trading with the Indians for furs. In 1807, he reached the Yellowstone region, with its stunning waterfalls and geysers. No one believed his reports of jets of steam that burst from the earth. Colter's stories sounded like the rambling tales of a man who had spent too many years alone in the mountains. William Clark took Colter seriously, however, and marked his

The Outpost on the Laramie

In 1834, fur trappers John Sublette and Robert Campbell established a trading post at the juncture of the Laramie and North Platte Rivers. They called it Fort William, but later changed the name to Fort Laramie. Fort Laramie was the first permanent white settlement in Wyoming. The U.S. Army took over Fort Laramie in 1849, and it served as a military outpost until 1890. Several buildings of the original fort have been restored at the Fort Laramie National Historic Site. An exhibit of authentic covered wagons offers visitors to the historic site a glimpse into the experience of the pioneers who crossed Wyoming on their way to Oregon and California during the 1840s and 1850s. ∎

route on a map he published in 1814. The northwestern corner of Wyoming came to be nicknamed "Colter's Hell."

Early in the nineteenth century, fur hats and cloaks were the height of fashion. The lustrous pelts of beavers and other fur-bearing animals brought high prices in New York, Paris, and London. The American Fur Company, based in Astoria, Oregon, and its agent in Wyoming—the Pacific Fur Company—needed a quick, secure route for transporting furs to eastern markets. In 1812, the company sent Robert Stuart in search of such a route through the

Rockies. In Wyoming, Stuart's expedition discovered South Pass, a 20-mile (32-km) opening through the mountains.

The discovery of South Pass was a boon to the fur industry. Trappers fanned out through the western mountains. Once a year, these "mountain men" gathered at an appointed rendezvous to exchange their furs for gunpowder, whiskey, and other goods. These meetings were noisy, rollicking affairs—the high point of the year for the lonely trappers. There was plenty of feasting and drinking, singing and cardplaying. By the last day, there were usually a few fights as well. When the fun was over, the trappers scattered into the mountains once more.

The mountain men encouraged the Native Americans to trap beavers and taught them how to stretch and dry the pelts. But there were never more than a few hundred of these white fur traders in Wyoming at any given time. For the most part, life for the Indians went on without major changes. They could scarcely have imagined how many white people lived across the plains to the east and what a crushing impact they would have when they began to head west by the thousands.

Jim Bridger, Master Scout

Born in Virginia, Jim Bridger (1804–1881) headed west as a boy and joined his first trapping expedition when he was eighteen. Over the decades that followed, Bridger explored a swath of country from the Missouri River to Utah and Idaho. He learned several Indian languages and served as a scout for the U.S. Army. He helped to establish Fort Bridger, a trading post in southwestern Wyoming. Like Fort Laramie, Fort Bridger became a military installation. It was shut down in 1890 with the closing of the frontier. ■

CHAPTER THREE

Westward Ho!

"We have done nothing but wade in the water, all day long. We have invented plans after plans, but to no purpose. We have stoned, hammered, and beat the oxen, but it was useless."

—Vincent Hoover, a pioneer on the Oregon Trail in 1849, describing his efforts to get his livestock across the North Platte near present-day Casper

Just Passing Through

In 1836, two young couples and two men followed a team of trappers through South Pass. The travelers were missionaries on their way to what is now the state of Washington. To reach their destination, they had to cross the desolate mountains and basins of Wyoming.

The Whitman party was in the forefront of a new westward movement. By 1840, thousands of families from the eastern states were setting off each year for the fertile land in the Pacific North-

Opposite: Settlers'
names carved on
Independence Rock
along the Oregon Trail

First Families

When missionary doctor Marcus Whitman (1802–1847) visited Wyoming in 1835, he found the Flathead and Nez Perce Indians receptive to his Christian message. He returned to his home in New York, married a young missionary named Narcissa Prentiss, and headed west to spread the Gospel on the Pacific Coast. Narcissa Prentiss Whitman (1808–1847) was one of the first women of European descent to cross the North American continent. For eleven years, the Whitmans worked at their mission in present-day Washington. They were both killed in 1847 when war broke out between the Indians and the white newcomers. ■

west. Their heavy wagons, packed with food, clothing, chickens, and children, lumbered along the Oregon Trail. Grown-ups and older children ran alongside, herding cows, horses, pigs, and sheep. The Oregon Trail followed the course of the North Platte River through Nebraska and into Wyoming. South Pass gave the travelers an easy route over the mountain ridge of the Great Divide.

Most settlers saw Wyoming as a barrier that separated them from their final destination. They did not marvel at its natural beauty, but

Mapping the Trails

Serving as a scout and mapmaker for the U.S. Army, John C. Frémont (1813–1890) explored much of the territory west of the Missouri River. In 1842, he mapped a route across Wyoming and explored the Wind River Mountain region. Frémont was a colorful character who made a fortune in the California gold rush. But he could not hold on to his money and lost his newfound wealth speculating on railroad companies. He helped seize California for the United States during the Mexican War (1846–1848) and is considered one of that state's founders. Frémont strongly opposed slavery and fought briefly for the Union in the Civil War (1861–1865). In the 1880s, he was appointed territorial governor of Arizona.

cursed its treeless plains and rugged, pitiless mountains. "This is a country that may captivate mad poets," wrote one traveler in 1846, "but I swear I see nothing but big rocks, high mountains, and wild sage. . . . It is a miserable country."

In 1847, another immigrant group, widely known as the Mormons, began to stream across Wyoming. The Mormons were followers of a new religious faith, the Church of Jesus Christ of Latter-day Saints. Brigham Young (1801–1877), the Mormon leader, founded a settlement in the Great Salt Lake valley in present-day

N

British Possessions

0 ____ 200 mi.
0 ____ 200 km

WASHINGTON, 1889

Columbia

Missouri

MONTANA, 1889

N. DAKOTA, 1889

MINN., 1858

OREGON, 1859

IDAHO, 1890

WYOMING, 1890

S. DAKOTA, 1889

NEBRASKA, 1867

CALIF., 1850

NEVADA, 1864

Colorado

Utah Territory

COLORADO, 1876

KANSAS, 1861

▭ Washington Territory, 1859–1863
▭ Dakota Territory, 1861–1863
▭ Nebraska Territory, 1861–1863
▭ State of Wyoming, 1890
▭ Other states, 1890
▭ U.S. territories, 1890

Arizona Territory

New Mexico Territory

Rio Grande

Unorganized Terr. until 1907

TEXAS, 1870

Historical map of Wyoming

A group of Mormons crossing the plains as they traveled to Salt Lake City, Utah

The Price of Privilege

In October 1856, two Mormon bands reached Wyoming. Most of the people in the Willie and Martin parties, as these groups are known today, were immigrants from the British Isles. They were too poor to own oxen or horses and transported their belongings on heavy handcarts. Caught in an early blizzard, the Willie and Martin parties became stranded near South Pass. Some 200 people died of hunger and cold. "The ravine was like an overcrowded tomb," a survivor recalled. "No mortal pen could describe the suffering." At last a rescue team arrived from Salt Lake City and escorted the survivors to Utah. "Was I sorry that I chose to come by handcart?" a survivor wrote years later. "No! Neither then nor one moment of my life! The price we paid to be acquainted with God was a privilege to pay." ∎

Utah. Thousands of Mormons from the eastern states and even from Europe rushed to Utah, which they regarded as the promised land of Zion. Like the Oregon pioneers, the Mormons followed the North Platte and crossed South Pass. There the Mormon Trail and the Oregon Trail diverged, and the Mormons headed southwest into Utah.

The year after Brigham Young reached Great Salt Lake, a ranch hand found a nugget of gold in northern California. By 1849 another wave of travelers stampeded west across Wyoming. The goldseekers were nicknamed forty-niners, because their westward rush began in 1849. Most of the forty-niners were young men who dreamed of making a quick fortune. They lived in terror that others would get to the goldfields ahead of them and scoop up all the wealth. As they crossed Wyoming, some forty-niners were in such a hurry that they discarded everything that weighed them

Equipped for seeking gold

down. They left behind their hammers, axes, grindstones, and trunks of clothing. Nothing mattered but their thirst for riches.

Earlier, Fort Laramie, Fort Bridger, and other outposts had served Wyoming's lonely fur trappers. In the 1840s, however, the U.S. Army took over these forts in an effort to protect and supply the hordes of newcomers. Busy markets grew up around the forts, selling sugar, flour, nails, whiskey, and other goods. Here and there, peddlers made their way up and down the trails, selling their wares to the travelers. But apart from the forts, Wyoming had virtually no permanent towns. It was not a place where people wanted to settle. Wyoming was merely a bleak stretch of trail on the way to greener pastures.

A Landmark on the Trail

On a scouting expedition in 1812, fur trader Robert Stuart saw an enormous granite boulder jutting from the meadows near present-day Casper. Since he sighted the boulder on the Fourth of July, he called it Independence Rock. Independence Rock (above) stands 193 feet (59 m) high and covers 27 acres (11 ha). It became a cherished landmark for pioneers on the Oregon Trail, who often paused to carve their names on its surface. When John C. Frémont passed the rock in 1842, he noted, "Everywhere within 6 or 8 feet [1.8 or 2.4 m] of the ground, and in some places 60 or 80 feet [18 or 24 m] above, the rock was inscribed with the names of travelers." Most of the names have been worn away by the elements now, but Independence Rock bears a plaque in honor of Narcissa Prentiss Whitman and Eliza Hart Spalding, the first white women to travel overland across North America. ■

Wyoming Territory

In the summer of 1867, a forest of tents and shacks sprouted on a patch of prairie in southeastern Wyoming. These makeshift shelters served as homes for the crew of workers who had come to lay gleaming railroad tracks across the plains. This lively "end-of-track town" was named Cheyenne in honor of the Cheyenne Indians. Four months after Cheyenne was founded, the first Union Pacific train chugged into the station. By that time, Cheyenne was a thriving metropolis of 6,000 people. Nearly all its inhabitants were men who worked for the railroad company. Women and children were all but unknown.

The railroad line that reached Cheyenne was one leg of a set of tracks destined to span the nation. This transcontinental railroad was completed in 1869 with a gala ceremony at Promontory Point, Utah. Now trains sped back and forth across Wyoming, pulled by mighty steam-powered engines. Trains stopped to refuel and pick up supplies at new towns that lay along the tracks like beads on a string: Cheyenne, Laramie, Benton, Green River, Bryan, Bear River City, and Evanston. Some of these towns dwindled and died when the crews moved on. But others clung to life, stubborn as the prairie grass around them.

Cheyenne became a bustling town when the Union Pacific Railroad built a station there.

The trains brought whites to Wyoming in numbers never seen before, and many came to stay. The Sioux and other Native Americans watched in horror as the newcomers slaughtered animals and staked claims on the land. To make matters worse, gold was discovered in Montana. A Montanan named J. M. Bozeman carved out a new trail that linked the Oregon Trail with the goldfields. This Bozeman Trail, opened in 1864, carried a stream of gold seekers through territory where few whites had ever ventured.

Red Cloud organized resistance to the Bozeman Trail.

The Sioux hated the Bozeman Trail and deeply resented Fort Phil Kearny, which the army erected for the trail's defense. Red Cloud, a respected Sioux chief and warrior, organized a fierce resistance. He and his war parties attacked anyone who left or approached the fort, killing some 150 white people within six months. At last, in 1868, the army abandoned the fort. The Fort Laramie Treaty gave the Indians the right to hunt bison in northeastern Wyoming. The region was given the status of "unceded Indian territory."

The Circle of Death

About 600 soldiers were stationed at Fort Phil Kearny in 1867, and twelve women, the wives of officers, also lived there. One of these women was Margaret Carrington, whose husband, Henry, was the post's commander.

In her diary, Margaret Carrington gives a vivid picture of life within the fort's walls. Measuring some 800 by 600 feet (244 by 183 m), the fort contained stables, warehouses, kitchens, a laundry, and an infirmary. The women often helped with the scrubbing and cooking. When they had free time, they played croquet, put on skits, or held dances.

Yet everyone knew that war parties waited outside. Margaret Carrington described the Sioux presence as a "circle of death." "Every day brought its probabilities of some Indian adventures," she wrote. "Every night had its special dangers which, unanticipated, might involve great loss." ■

When the railroad crews set to work in 1867, Wyoming was part of a U.S. territory called Dakota. This sprawling territory had been created in 1861 and included most of Wyoming and what is now North and South Dakota. Wyoming's boomtowns made the settlers in eastern Dakota Territory uneasy. They feared that Wyomingites would control the territorial legislature. In 1868, a delegation from eastern Dakota petitioned the U.S. Congress to divide the territory. Wyoming was created from the western half of this great tract of land. A bit of territory was added from the edges of Utah and Idaho, making Wyoming a perfect rectangle. Wyoming became a U.S. territory in 1868.

A wagon train passing through Dakota Territory

Women voting in Cheyenne during the 1880s

"The Same under the Law"

The first legislature of Wyoming Territory convened at Cheyenne in October 1869. At that time, Wyoming had only about 8,000 people, most of them living in tiny towns along the railroad line. Yet, within two months, this remote territory passed a law that was unique in the history of the world. It granted women the right to vote and to hold elected office on an equal basis with men. The law proclaimed, "Every woman of the age of twenty-one years residing in this territory, may at every election to be holden under the laws thereof, cast her vote. And her rights to the elective franchise and to hold office shall be the same under the election laws of the territory, as those of electors." Governor John A. Campbell signed the bill into law on December 10, 1869.

Why did Wyoming take such a radical step? Certainly, some of the legislators had a deep conviction that the voting act was right and just, but another compelling reason was Wyoming's eagerness to grow. The territory had very few women, and Wyomingites hoped that more would emigrate. Perhaps women would come to Wyoming if it promised freedom that was not granted anywhere else.

Though Wyoming sought to treat women fairly, it had few such concerns for the rights of its Native Americans. In 1869, the Shoshone were forced to move onto the Wind River Reservation,

The Wind River Reservation, where many Shoshone were forced to move in 1869

The Mother of Woman Suffrage

Wyoming Territory held its first election in 1870. The voters of South Pass City (now a ghost town) selected Esther H. Morris to serve as justice of the peace. Esther Morris (1814–1902) was the first woman in the world ever elected to such a position. Little is known about her life, but the records show that she served for eight months and tried fifty cases. The suffragist leader Susan B. Anthony referred to her as "the Mother of Woman Suffrage." ■

about 100 miles (161 km) north of the railroad line. And despite the Fort Laramie Treaty, the "unceded Indian territory" in northeastern Wyoming was soon in the hands of white settlers. In 1877, the last Sioux and Arapaho were driven out of Wyoming and sent to a reservation in present-day South Dakota. The following year an Arapaho band petitioned to join the Shoshone at Wind River. The request was granted. Those Shoshone and Arapaho, about 2,000 people in all, were the only Indians left in all of Wyoming Territory.

Over the next twenty years, Wyoming's population grew almost eightfold and Wyomingites prepared to ask Congress for statehood. In 1889, fifty-five delegates met in Cheyenne to draw up a state constitution. Ironically, no women served on that committee, but under the proposed state constitution, women retained their right to vote.

When Congress considered statehood for Wyoming, woman suffrage was a major issue. Many congressmen (all representatives and senators at that time were male) argued that women did not have the "capacity to vote wisely." They suggested that Wyoming

Wyoming's Constitutional Convention of 1889

might set a bad example for other states by allowing women to vote. Despite these arguments, however, the bill to grant statehood to Wyoming passed in both the House and the Senate, and President Benjamin Harrison signed it into law. On July 10, 1890, Wyoming became the forty-fourth state in the Union.

Wyoming's statehood was a victory for champions of women's rights. An 1891 woman suffrage convention proclaimed, "Wyoming, all hail; the first true republic the world has ever seen."

CHAPTER FOUR

Taming the Land

My foot's in the stirrup, I'm a-leavin' Cheyenne,
My pony won't stand, I'm off to Montan'.
Good-bye, Old Paint, I'm a-leavin' Cheyenne!
Good-bye, Old Paint, I'm a-leavin' Cheyenne.
With my feet in the stirrups I'm off to Montana,
Good-bye, Old Paint, I'm a-leavin' Cheyenne.

—One of the oldest and best-known cowboy songs of Wyoming
("Old Paint" is a term referring to a pinto horse.)

Raising cattle was big business in Wyoming by the late 1800s.

Boots and Spurs

By the 1870s, Texas was famous for its own breed of cattle, the Texas longhorn. The longhorn had a spread of curving horns measuring up to 6 feet (1.8 m) from tip to tip. In the years after the Civil War, the demand for beef increased, and Texas ranchers saw the chance to make huge profits. But the Texas plains did not provide

Opposite: A field of sage in summer

enough grass to feed their growing herds, so the ranchers began to look north for better grazing land.

Eastern Wyoming and Montana had fierce, icy winters, but when the snow melted, the land sprouted a thick carpet of tall grasses. Texas ranchers herded their animals north each spring and let them fatten on the prairie grasses. From there, the cattle were driven to rail terminals and shipped to market. Eventually some ranchers discovered "winter grazing," keeping their cattle in the north year-round. By 1884, some 800,000 head of cattle were grazing on the Wyoming plains.

Cattle drives on the Texas Trail, roundups on the range, branding days, and thundering stampedes—all became part of the Wyoming mystique. The legend of the Wyoming cowboy has

The cowboy life was perceived to be adventurous and free.

Devils Tower

One landmark for cowherders in the Belle Fourche Valley was a hauntingly beautiful pillar of rock known as Devils Tower. Devils Tower, 10 miles (16 km) south of Hulett, was formed millions of years ago when an extinct volcano eroded away, leaving only a central core of twisted lava. The tower rises 867 feet (264 m) above its base. According to a Sioux legend, the deep grooves on its sides are the claw marks of giant bears. The bears climbed up the tower in pursuit of several young girls who had been gathering flowers. Finally the bears fell from the rock and were killed. The girls made ropes with their flowers and descended safely.

In 1906, President Theodore Roosevelt preserved this unique landmark for future generations. Devils Tower became the first national monument in the United States. Today, it is familiar to moviegoers the world over. In the 1977 film *Close Encounters of the Third Kind*, humans and extraterrestrials come face-to-face at Devils Tower in a climactic final scene. ■

inspired novels and songs, paintings, movies, and TV series. Cowhands were seen as free spirits who worked and lived under the open sky. They hated towns and fences and loved to ride for days on the open range. The cowboy mystique sprang up at a time when America's frontier had all but disappeared. Most Americans still lived in rural areas, but each year more people moved to cities and towns. Only the cowboy still seemed to live a life of adventure and freedom.

In reality, however, herding cattle was hard, dirty work. Cows are not the most intelligent animals, and their dispositions are far from sweet. When frightened, they charge wildly, mowing down anyone who gets in their way. Wyoming cowboys spent months at a time among these mooing, sweating beasts, sleeping on the

Robin Hood on the Range

The English outlaw Robin Hood was said to steal from the rich and give to the poor. The Wyoming outlaw Butch Cassidy (1866–1908) earned a similar reputation. Born George Leroy Parker, Cassidy robbed banks and stagecoaches and often shared his ill-gotten gains with widows and orphans. It was said that he never killed anyone on purpose. Cassidy's "Wild Bunch" gang was centered in the town of Kaycee. ■

ground and seldom bathing. When they reached a town, their chief entertainment was drinking and gambling. It was a lonely life, far from the comforts of home and family.

At its best, cattle raising was a highly profitable business for the rancher. The cost of raising a steer for three years was about $4.50 and a three-year-old steer could sell for as much as $40 at the slaughterhouse.

But ranching on the Wyoming plains posed many problems. Cougars and grizzlies often carried off young calves. A major drought or an especially harsh winter could wipe out a whole herd. And then there was the problem of cattle rustling. Rustlers, or cattle thieves, rounded up wandering cows and changed their brands. It was hard for the original owner to find a stolen animal or to prove that it belonged to him.

In the course of a year, a single steer needed as much as 30 acres (12 ha) of grazing land. A large herd, therefore, required a ranch of several thousand acres. Wealthy Texans owned most of Wyoming's large ranches. But by the 1890s, smaller stockmen tried to enter the business as well. The big ranchers, or "cattle barons," deeply resented the newcomers. They claimed that the small ranchers were rustlers who stole their animals. Fences were another source of conflict. The new ranchers often put up fences to keep their small landholdings from being grazed by neighbors' cattle. The cattle barons, however, were used to having an open range where their animals could graze freely.

The struggles between large-scale and small-scale ranchers sometimes flared into violence. The cattle barons did not wait for the law to deal with suspected rustlers. They took matters into their

The Johnson County War

Based in Cheyenne, the Wyoming Stock Growers Association (WSGA) represented the most powerful ranchers in the state. When small ranchers in and around Johnson County formed a rival organization, the WSGA went into action. In April 1892, a special train pulled into Casper carrying horses, three supply wagons, several ranch foremen, and twenty professional gunmen from Texas. Like a military battalion, the group headed for Johnson County. The Texans, calling themselves the Invaders, killed two suspected rustlers in their cabin after a daylong siege. The Invaders then took shelter at the TA Ranch near the town of Buffalo. They were finally captured by federal troops from Cheyenne. The Invaders, who were released on bail, then fled back to Texas, and they were never tried for their crimes. ■

own hands. Many a small rancher was "dry-gulched"—murdered on the prairie and thrown into a dry ravine.

Cattle ranchers and sheep ranchers also had serious clashes. Sheep cropped the grass almost down to its roots, leaving nothing for cows to eat. Cattle ranchers accused the sheep raisers of ruining good land. In retaliation, cattle ranchers sometimes killed sheep, or "woolies," and even murdered sheepherders. The strife between sheep ranchers and cattle ranchers led to many bloody skirmishes from about 1900 to 1910.

Using the Land

In the early days of statehood, ranching was not Wyoming's only industry. Southern Wyoming had rich veins of subbituminous coal. Subbituminous coal is a variety of soft coal that produces low amounts of sulfur when it burns. The Union Pacific Railroad opened coal mines in Campbell, Uinta, Sweetwater, and Carbon Counties to supply fuel for its locomotives. The railroad also hauled Wyoming coal to markets in other parts of the country. By the late 1880s, about 2,000 Wyomingites worked in the coal industry.

A coal mine in Carbon County, 1896

The Rock Springs Massacre

Wyomingites of European heritage deeply resented the Chinese immigrants who came to work in the coal mines. Because the Chinese refused to strike for higher pay, other workers felt that they kept wages down. Anti-Chinese feeling flared in 1885, when British and Swedish miners attacked a group of Chinese near the town of Rock Springs. Twenty-eight Chinese miners were killed, fifteen were injured, and hundreds were forced to flee for their lives. The state governor asked for federal troops to help keep the peace. For the next thirteen years, armed soldiers remained in Rock Springs. The governor claimed they were there to protect the miners, but actually the troops stayed in Rock Springs to protect the interests of the powerful Union Pacific Railroad, which preferred to hire low-paid Chinese laborers. ■

Most of the first coal miners were immigrants from Great Britain and Sweden. The work was hard and dangerous, and the pay was low—only five cents per bushel of coal. In 1875, miners organized a strike to demand higher wages. Most of the strikers were fired and forced to leave the state. The railroads replaced them with Chinese miners, who were willing to work for only four cents a bushel.

In the deep and narrow tunnels of the mines, workers breathed air that was full of coal dust. Many miners developed a deadly illness called black lung disease. Others died when mineshafts caved in, or when fires broke out underground. In 1903, 171 men were killed in a mine disaster at Hanna, Wyoming. Another fifty-eight men died in the same mine five years later.

Early trappers in Wyoming sometimes saw a thick black substance seeping from cracks between the rocks. They knew that this oil, or "black tar," burned well. But no one found a way to mine the oil until the 1880s. In 1883, Wyoming's first oil well was drilled at Dallas Field near the town of Lander. Wyoming's most productive fields proved to be those at Salt Creek north of Casper. Casper opened its first oil refinery in 1894. Horse-drawn wagons loaded with barrels hauled crude oil to the refinery from the Salt Creek wells.

At first, most of Wyoming's oil was used by the Union Pacific Railroad. Demand soared, however, with the popularity of the automobile. Oil was no longer "black tar"; by the early 1900s, it was "black gold." No longer did horse-drawn wagons haul barrels of crude oil from the wellheads. A web of pipelines now carried it to the refinery. Casper mushroomed into a thriving metropolis

The town of Casper thrived because of the oil in nearby fields.

with fancy restaurants and glittering hotels designed for the rich and the would-be rich.

Wyoming's oil industry received a fresh boost when the United States entered World War I in 1917. But as the United States slid into the devastating economic depression of the 1930s, fuel prices fell. A severe drought made Wyoming's plight even worse. Its once-prized grazing land turned into a semidesert. Wyoming's economy revived when the United States entered World War II in 1941. War plants burned coal night and day, and oil was in demand to fuel trains, tanks, and aircraft. Wyoming's stores of fossil fuel made a significant contribution to America's war effort.

Scandal at Teapot Dome

In 1910, President William Howard Taft set aside the oil field called Teapot Dome (left) as a reserve for the Navy Department. In 1921, however, President Warren G. Harding secretly transferred the oil field to the Department of the Interior. Secretary of the Interior Albert B. Fall was Harding's close friend. In another secret arrangement, Fall leased Teapot Dome to his friend Harry Sinclair, head of the Sinclair Oil Company. Sinclair organized a new company named Mammoth Oil Company to take on the lease.

Teapot Dome proved to be the biggest "gusher" in Wyoming history. The oil field's fame led to investigations, and all the secret transactions came to light. The public was shocked by such misconduct on the part of the president and one of his top officials. Albert Fall was convicted of bribery and received a one-year sentence and a $100,000 fine—he was the first U.S. cabinet secretary ever to go to prison. Warren Harding died before the scandal broke, so he was never charged for his part in the affair. ■

Seeking the Balance

The end of World War II in 1945 launched the world into a frightening new era, sometimes called the Atomic Age. For the first time in history, people had the power to build nuclear weapons, weapons of mass destruction. Uranium was a crucial ingredient for creating nuclear reactions. In the years after the war, scientists and fortune hunters combed the country searching for deposits of this valuable mineral. Important uranium reserves were found in the basins of the Powder, Shirley, and Wind Rivers. For a few years Wyoming experienced a uranium boom, not unlike the oil boom of the 1920s.

Despite these activities, Wyoming's population was still very small compared to that of other states. Wyoming's vast stretches of undeveloped land seemed ideally suited to military installations. In 1960, intercontinental ballistic missiles were put in place at F. E. Warren Air Force Base near Cheyenne. Warren was the first U.S. base to house these powerful weapons. Minuteman missiles were put into position around Cheyenne in 1965.

Wyoming's petroleum industry got a boost in the early 1970s, when the United States faced a serious oil shortage. Wyoming's population jumped almost 42 percent between 1970 and 1980. This rapid growth trailed off after 1980, when other sources of petroleum were again more available.

An eroded hillside resulting from extensive uranium mining

In the 1970s, some Wyomingites grew concerned that mining, grazing, and the military were exploiting the land. They argued that Wyoming's pristine landscape is its greatest resource, and that it should be protected from ruthless development. Other voices disagreed, calling for new industry to bring money and jobs into the state.

One of Wyoming's most vital industries is tourism, which relies on the preservation of the state's natural wonders. The tourist industry began in 1872 with the founding of Yellowstone National Park and continues to flourish and grow, providing hundreds of jobs and bringing billions of dollars to the state. Most tourists come from out of state. For a week or

two, they explore Yellowstone or Grand Teton and visit a few of the state's Western history museums. Then they return home or move on to tourist attractions in neighboring states. Like the wagon-train travelers of long ago, they are only passing through.

Tourists travel from all over the world to visit Grand Teton National Park and other Wyoming attractions.

CHAPTER FIVE

High, Wide, and Lonesome

Wildflowers set
against the backdrop
of the Grand Tetons

"Today the sun is out, only a few clouds billowing. In the east, where the sheep have started off without me, the benchland tilts up in a series of eroded red earth mesas planed flat on top by a million years of water. Behind them a bold line of muscular scarps rears up 10,000 feet [3,050 m] to become the Bighorn Mountains. A tidal pattern is engraved into the ground as if left by the sea that once covered the state. Canyons curve down like galaxies to meet the oncoming rush of flat land."

—Gretel Ehrlich, a Wyoming writer and sheepherder

The High Plateau

Wyoming is a nearly perfect rectangle, carved from the high plateau country of the Great Plains and the northern Rocky Mountains. At its lowest point—the Belle Fourche River in Crook County—Wyoming's land lies 3,099 feet (945 m) above sea level.

Opposite: Wyoming's
Great Divide

Wyoming's topography

Gannett Peak, the highest point in the state, towers 13,804 feet (4,210 m). On average, the land in Wyoming is 6,700 feet (2,044 m) above sea level, making Wyoming one of the highest states in the nation, second only to Colorado.

Sprawling over 97,819 square miles (253,351 square kilometers), Wyoming is ninth largest among the fifty states. Its neighbor to the north is Montana, which bends around the state's northwestern corner. Idaho and Utah lie to the west. Utah and Colorado form Wyoming's southern border. To the east are Nebraska and South Dakota.

The eastern third of Wyoming is the western edge of a vast North American land feature called the Great Plains. The Great Plains is a high, nearly treeless region, which was once covered with tall grasses. Wyoming's plains region provides excellent grazing land for cattle and sheep, but the land is too poor for growing most crops.

The Black Hills are a range of low mountains—about 6,000 feet (1,830 m) on average—rising from the plains in northeastern Wyoming and extending into South Dakota. The hills are covered with ponderosa pines, which gives them a darkish tint when seen from a distance. In actuality, the Black Hills are surprisingly green for this relatively dry part of the country. The plains in Wyoming

Riding the Gangplank

Rising from the Great Plains in southeastern Wyoming is a narrow finger of land known as the Gangplank. Shaped like the gangplank of a ship, this unusual land feature is only about 100 yards (92 m) across. The Gangplank climbs gradually into the Laramie Mountains. Many years ago, crews built the Union Pacific Railroad along the Gangplank into the mountains. ■

are also broken by the Laramie Mountains to the south. West of Cheyenne, the plains give way to a series of jagged mountain ranges, part of the Rocky Mountain region that stretches from Canada to Mexico. Wyoming's ranges include the Bighorn, Absaroka, and Wind River in the north, and the Teton, Gros Ventre, Salt River, and Snake River Ranges in the west. Farther south stand the Medicine Bow Mountains and the Sierra Madre.

Wyoming's third major landform is the intermontane basin. Several of these basins are found throughout the state. As the name suggests, these basins are deep, bowl-shaped depressions ringed by mountains. Intermontane basins are often called "holes"

Within the Great Divide

In southwestern Wyoming, a ridge known as the Great Divide forms a ring around a deep, arid hole—the Great Divide Basin. This vast, round valley spreads over 3,000 square miles (7,770 sq km) and has no lakes or rivers for drainage. Rainwater is simply absorbed by the thirsty soil. ■

in Wyoming. Among the largest basins are Bighorn and Powder River Basins in the north; Wind River Basin in central Wyoming; and Washakie, Green River, and Great Divide Basins in the south. Hell's Half Acre is a 320-acre (130-ha) basin west of Casper where wind and water have created otherworldly towers, ridges, and gullies of sculpted stone.

Zigzagging from the northwest corner of Wyoming to its south-central border is a ridge of mountains known as the Continental Divide. Rivers that rise west of the Continental Divide flow to the Pacific Ocean. Rivers that begin east of the divide flow to the Atlantic Ocean and the Gulf of Mexico.

Fishing along the Snake River

Wyoming's Geographical Features

Total area; rank	97,819 sq. mi. (253,351 sq km); 9th
Land; rank	97,105 sq. mi. (251,502 sq km); 9th
Water; rank	714 sq. mi. (1,849 sq km); 35th
Inland water; **rank**	714 sq. mi. (1,849 sq km); 30th
Geographic center	Fremont, 58 miles (93 km) northeast of Lander
Highest point	Gannett Peak, 13,804 feet (4,210 m)
Lowest point	Belle Fourche River in Crook County, 3,099 feet (945 m)
Largest city	Cheyenne
Population; rank	455,975 (1990 census); 50th
Record high temperature	114°F (46°C) at Basin on July 12, 1900
Record low temperature	–63°F (–53°C) at Moran, near Elk, on February 9, 1933
Average July temperature	67°F (19°C)
Average January temperature	19°F (–7°C)
Average annual precipitation	13 inches (33 cm)

Most Wyoming rivers are small, but they feed some of the mightiest river systems on the continent. The Green River, flowing south across western Wyoming into Utah, is a major branch of the Colorado. The Snake River flows through Yellowstone and Grand Teton National Parks before it turns west to join the Columbia. The Platte, Yellowstone, Belle Fourche, Bighorn, Sweetwater, and Powder Rivers pour their waters into the Missouri, which in turn joins the Mississippi. Yellowstone Lower Falls plunges 308 feet (94 m) into the magnificent Grand Canyon of the Yellowstone.

Wyoming has few natural lakes. The largest and best known is Yellowstone Lake, noted for its beauty and its large trout. Lying 7,731 feet (2,358 m) above sea level, it is the highest lake in the United States. Other Wyoming lakes include Frémont, Jackson, de Smet, and Shoshone. In addition, damming and diverting rivers have created many reservoirs. These artificial lakes are used for

Lower Yellowstone Falls

both recreation and irrigation. Among Wyoming's reservoirs are Seminoe, Pathfinder, Buffalo Bill, Boysen, and Big Sandy.

At the Mercy of the Elements

"During the winter it does not snow much, we being above snow line," wrote the Wyoming humorist Bill Nye in 1881. "But in the summer the snow clouds rise above us, and thus the surprised and indignant agriculturist is caught in the middle of a July day with a terrific fall of snow, so he is virtually compelled to wear his snowshoes all through his haying season."

Wyoming weather is the stuff tall tales are made of. Winter temperatures of −30° Fahrenheit (−34° Celsius) are not uncommon, and sometimes the mercury hovers in those depths for days on end. Describing an especially bitter winter, Wyoming writer Gretel Ehrlich says, "To say you were snowed in didn't express the problem. You were either 'froze in,' 'froze up,' or 'froze out,' depending

A Jackson ranch covered in snow

The Year That Broke the Barons

A disastrous drought struck the Wyoming plains in the summer of 1887. Desperate cattle wandered into towns in search of water and food. This terrible summer was followed by one of the worst winters in Wyoming's history. Thousands of cattle froze to death when one fierce blizzard followed another. In the course of this catastrophic year, many of Wyoming's cattle barons lost their herds and were driven to financial ruin. ■

Summer weather in Wyoming attracts those who love the outdoors.

on where your pickup or your legs stopped working." Wyoming's record low temperature was –63°F (–53°C), on February 9, 1933, at Moran. The average January temperature is 19°F (–7°C).

Summers vary, depending upon the altitude. Temperatures remain pleasantly cool in the mountains but can be broiling in

low-lying regions. On July 12, 1900, the temperature reached a record 114°F (46°C) at Basin. The average July temperature is 67°F (19°C).

With an average annual precipitation of only 13 inches (33 centimeters), Wyoming is a very dry state. Rainfall is sparse in the basins and on the eastern plains but occurs more frequently at higher altitudes. Snowfall is heavy in the mountains, especially in the Tetons and Absarokas. Mountain passes are usually closed from October to May, due to the threat of avalanches.

Refuge from Starvation

During the winter, forage is scarce for elk and other large game animals. At Wyoming's National Elk Refuge, some 8,000 elk are offered food and protection each winter. Founded in 1912, the refuge covers 24,700 acres (10,000 ha) near Jackson, Wyoming. By feeding elk at the refuge, the government discourages them from foraging at nearby farms. ■

A Pleasuring-Ground for the People

Yellowstone National Park rests upon a "hot spot," an area where molten rock, or magma, from the Earth's core seethes toward the surface. Groundwater seeps down through cracks in the rock, heats to the boiling point, and bursts forth in jets of steam called geysers. In other places, minerals color bubbling ponds of mud known as paint pots. In addition to these natural wonders, the Yellowstone region has areas of remote wilderness that provide a habitat for many threatened and endangered species. Yellowstone National Park was created in 1872 by an act of Congress, as "a pleasuring-ground for the benefit and enjoyment of the people." ■

Wild Wyoming

Some 11,000 years ago, humans followed the animals they hunted into Wyoming. They followed big game such as mammoths and giant bison, creatures whose meat could feed a family for many weeks. About 200 years ago, Wyoming's animals lured another wave of immigrants—the European fur trappers. The beaver, mink, fox, and other small furry creatures played a major role in the state's history. Wyoming is still rich in animal life, though some species have vanished, and many others are found in dwindling numbers.

One of Wyoming's most beautiful animals is the swift, graceful pronghorn. Pronghorns roam the plains in small herds, often consisting of one male with several females and their young. When the pronghorn runs, its white rump flashes a danger signal to the rest of the group. Other hoofed animals in the state include moose, elk, bighorn sheep, and mule deer. A small herd of bison lives in Yellowstone National Park.

When Wyoming became a U.S. territory, the settlers made war on the timber wolf. Wolves disappeared from the state by the early twentieth century. Since then, they have been occasionally sighted in Yellowstone. In 1995, environmentalists reintroduced them to the park, although many people protested the move. Yellowstone is also the last home of the mighty grizzly in Wyoming. The coyote, the wolf's smaller cousin, is found in most parts of the state, and black bears live in many mountainous areas. Another large predator is the mountain lion, or cougar. Though it is rarely seen, its eerie cry can sometimes be heard on still mountain nights.

Coyotes can be found throughout Wyoming.

Wyoming's smaller mammals include the beaver, mink, otter, raccoon, skunk, and fox. The rare black-footed ferret, a member of the weasel family, also survives here. Gophers and ground squirrels dig burrows on the plains. The plains are also an ideal habitat for cottontails and jackrabbits.

Gone, but Not Forgotten

One day in the early 1880s, a railroad worker discovered an empty cabin near Como Bluff, not far from the town of Medicine Bow. To his amazement, the cabin was built entirely of gigantic bones. Scientists rushed to Wyoming to study this strange find. The bones belonged to dinosaurs that had roamed the area millions of years ago. The region proved to be rich in dinosaur fossils. Two scientists, one from the Peabody Museum at Yale University and the other from the Academy of Sciences in Philadelphia, waged a virtual war over the dinosaur bones for more than a decade. They slandered each other in print and even stole each other's specimens. To this day no one knows who built the mysterious bone cabin, but it is still standing at Como Bluff. ■

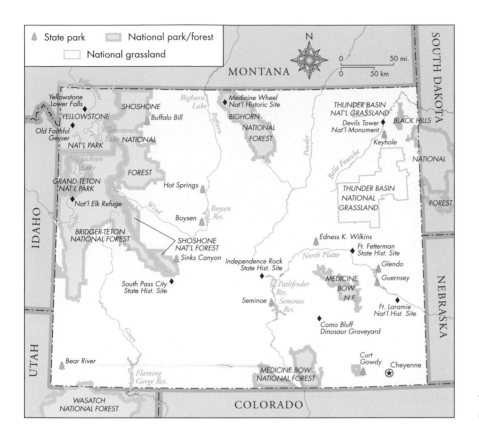

Map legend:
- ▲ State park
- National park/forest
- National grassland

N

MONTANA

SOUTH DAKOTA

0 — 50 mi.
0 — 50 km

Yellowstone
Lower Falls
YELLOWSTONE
Old Faithful
Geyser
NAT'L PARK
Yellowstone Lake
Jackson Lake
GRAND TETON
NAT'L PARK
Nat'l Elk Refuge
Snake
BRIDGER-TETON
NATIONAL FOREST

SHOSHONE
Buffalo Bill
NATIONAL
FOREST
Hot Springs
Wind
Boysen
Boysen Res.
SHOSHONE
NAT'L FOREST
Sinks Canyon
South Pass City
State Hist. Site

Bighorn Lake
Medicine Wheel
Nat'l Historic Site
BIGHORN
NATIONAL
FOREST
Bighorn
Powder

Independence Rock
State Hist. Site
Pathfinder Res.
Seminoe
Seminoe Res.

THUNDER BASIN
NAT'L GRASSLAND
Devils Tower
Nat'l Monument
BLACK HILLS
Keyhole
NATIONAL
Belle Fourche
THUNDER BASIN
NATIONAL
GRASSLAND
FOREST

Edness K. Wilkins
Ft. Fetterman
State Hist. Site
North Platte
Glendo
Guernsey
MEDICINE
BOW
N.F.
Ft. Laramie
Nat'l Hist. Site

NEBRASKA

Como Bluff
Dinosaur Graveyard

Bear River
Green
Flaming Gorge Res.
MEDICINE BOW
NATIONAL FOREST

Curt
Gowdy
Cheyenne ✪

IDAHO

UTAH

WASATCH
NATIONAL FOREST

COLORADO

**Wyoming's parks
and forests**

Wyoming is home to many birds of prey, including the bald eagle and golden eagle. Among the state's songbirds are the lark bunting, Bullock's oriole, long-tailed chat, and western mockingbird. The lakes and reservoirs attract several duck species in the summer months.

About one-sixth of Wyoming's land is covered with forests. Three national forests exist wholly within Wyoming: Shoshone, Bighorn, and Medicine Bow. Black Hills National Forest extends into Wyoming from South Dakota, and Bridger-Teton National Forest spills across the border into Idaho. Loggers

Shoshone National Forest

harvest Douglas fir, Engelmann spruce, lodgepole pine, and ponderosa pine.

Wyoming's plains have few trees, though cottonwoods and aspens grow along rivers and streams. When the first white people arrived, the plains were a rippling sea of grasses that sometimes grew as tall as a man. The tallest of these grasses were needlegrass and bluestem, while shorter species included grama, buffalo grass, bluegrass, and wheatgrass. Today these native grasses have largely been replaced by European varieties.

A forest of lodgepole pines

Getting Back to Nature

Thunder Basin National Grassland is a 2-million-acre (810,000-ha) swath of prairie in the Platte River valley of eastern Wyoming. Operated by the federal Bureau of Land Management (BLM), it is one of the last tracts of original prairie in the United States. Grazing, mining, and even archaeological excavations are carefully controlled. Here needlegrass, bluestem, and other native prairie grasses still ripple like the waves of the sea. ■

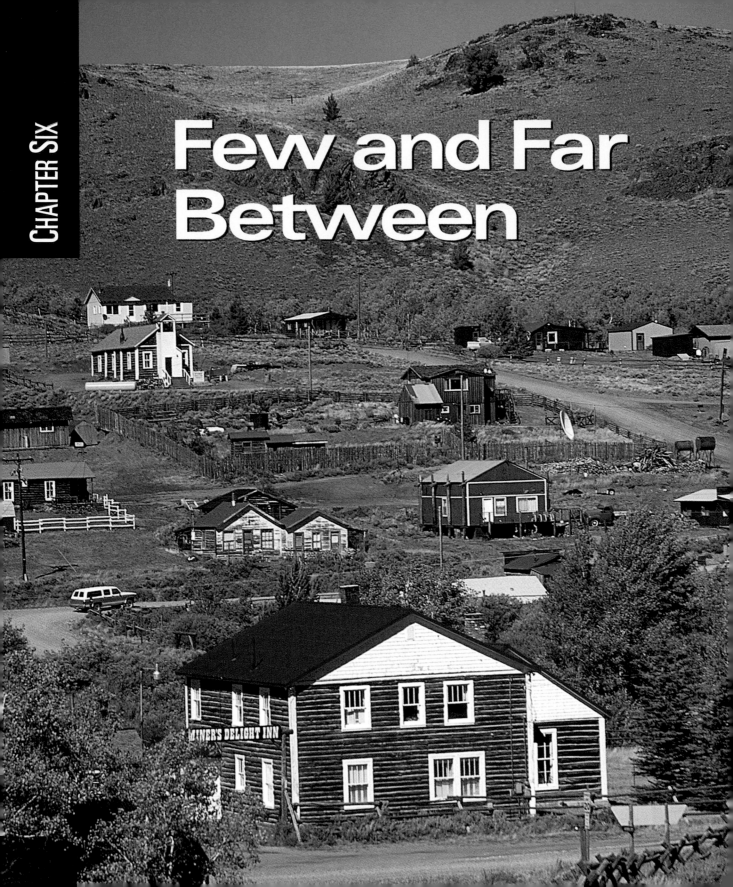

CHAPTER SIX

Few and Far Between

If you are driving south from Gillette, Wyoming, you will travel 38 miles (61 km) before you reach the next town, the tiny crossroads village of Reno Junction. From Reno Junction to the town of Bill is another 40 miles (64 km). The next town, Douglas, is 35 miles (56 km) farther still along the same empty highway. Wyoming's towns and small cities are sprinkled lightly across the map, separated by wide stretches of uninhabited land.

The town of Douglas is situated along a lonely highway.

The Eastern Plain

Eastern Wyoming is a high rolling prairie—the western edge of North America's Great Plains. This is cattle country, and most of its towns grew up as supply centers for the ranchers. While the scenery can be monotonous, many parts of the plain are broken by foothills and mountains.

Opposite: An inn near South Pass

A statue of Esther Hobart Morris stands near the entrance of the capitol in Cheyenne.

Cheyenne, the Capital City

Cheyenne has been Wyoming's capital since territorial days. Though it has only 50,000 people, it is Wyoming's largest city. A major downtown landmark is the golden dome of the state capitol. A statue of Esther Hobart Morris, the world's first elected woman justice of the peace, stands beside the capitol's main entrance. Plaques in the central rotunda honor famous Wyoming governors including Francis E. Warren, Joseph M. Carey, and John B. Kendrick. Climbing to the dome, the visitor is greeted by mounted specimens of Wyoming wildlife, including a cougar, a bison, and an elk.

Cheyenne was founded in 1867 by the Union Pacific Railroad and soon became a depot for transporting cattle to market. At roundup time, Cheyenne overflowed with cowhands. They drank, gambled, and often got into fights. One eyewitness commented, "Hell must have been raked to furnish the inhabitants, and to hell they must return after graduating there." Today, little remains of Cheyenne's rip-roaring early days. But the old Union Pacific depot is now the Railroad Museum, tracing the colorful history of the transcontinental railroad that helped to build the state.

Wyoming has many museums on Western history. The most extensive of them all is the Wyoming State Museum in Cheyenne.

Its collections include Native American crafts, early paintings and photographs, railroad memorabilia, and cowboy equipment such as saddles, spurs, and lariats.

The old Union Pacific depot in Cheyenne is now a museum.

Laramie

West of Cheyenne, where the prairie breaks into the wooded Snowy Range of the Medicine Bow Mountains, lies the city of Laramie. The city was named for French trapper Jacques La Ramie, who was killed by Indians around 1820. Almost nothing is known about La Ramie's life, but a city and a river bear his name today.

Register Cliff

Not far from the town of Guernsey is Register Cliff, a striking relic of the Oregon Trail. On this sheer white precipice above the North Platte River, hundreds of pioneers stopped to carve their names. Deep ruts left by processions of heavy wagons can still be seen on the prairie today. ■

Laramie is the home of the University of Wyoming, the only four-year university in the state. Magnificent spruce trees shelter its dorms and classroom buildings. The pride of the university campus is the six-story Centennial Center. Built in the form of a tepee, the Centennial Center contains a concert hall and an array of museums and galleries. Within this complex is the University Art Museum, with some 6,000 paintings and sculptures from around the world.

Another Laramie attraction is the Ivinson Mansion. During Wyoming's early days, the mansion belonged to Edward Ivinson, an Englishman who made a fortune selling railroad ties to the Union Pacific. Also known as the Laramie Plains Museum, the Ivinson Mansion has been restored to portray life among the well-to-do in the late nineteenth century. Visitors can explore the kitchen, children's nursery, parlors, and even the bathroom.

The University of Wyoming is located in Laramie.

North of Cheyenne is the town of Torrington. Torrington owes its prosperity not to cattle, but to sugar beets. The Homesteaders Museum depicts life among farmers on the Great Plains. Many artifacts and photographs on display came from the nearby 4A Ranch.

Gillette lies in the shadow of the Black Hills in parched, treeless northeastern Wyoming. The region is rich in deposits of petroleum and low-sulfur coal. Strip-mining has left its scars on much of the surrounding land. But fossil fuels have also brought prosperity to Gillette, which has one of the best school systems in the state. Gillette students even have their own planetarium.

Laramie's Ivinson Mansion

Into the Rockies

West of the plains the land breaks into a series of mountain ranges. These ranges are all part of the great Rocky Mountain chain. The rugged landscape makes grazing difficult, but mining and tourism are important industries.

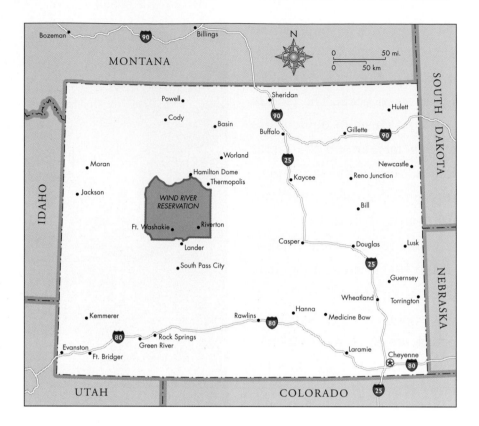

Wyoming's cities and interstates

Casper

The city of Casper lies almost at the center of Wyoming. Casper began as an oil boomtown in 1890, and oil is still the main industry in the area. During the winter, Casper draws skiers from all over the United States. In the summer months, locals enjoy swimming and boating at the nearby Pathfinder, Alcova, and Seminoe Reservoirs.

Other Mountain Towns

Buffalo was not named for the bison of the plains, but for the city in western New York, early home of one of the town's founders.

Once Butch Cassidy and his Wild Bunch frequented Buffalo's saloons. Today Buffalo recalls its colorful past at the Jim Gatchell Historical Society and Museum. Among the museum's

Casper's economy is still based on the oil industry.

Home on the Range

In the early 1880s, Moreton Frewen and his brother Richard set up a cattle ranch in Wyoming's Powder River country. Its main house resembled a hunting lodge on a British estate and was known as Castle Frewen. The Frewens loved to host extravagant parties for cattle barons and their families. No luxury was too expensive for their guests. They even had hothouse roses delivered by stagecoach or rail from faraway Denver as corsages for the ladies. The Frewens lost their fortune in the terrible winter of 1887–1888, and the famous parties came to an abrupt end. ■

displays is a collection of photographs of the Castle Frewen, built on the range by two English brothers in the early 1880s.

Many of Wyoming's cattle barons built elegant homes in Sheridan. Today, several of these mansions still stand on Sheridan's main street. The 1913 home of rancher and Wyoming governor John B. Kendrick is surrounded by gardens. On the grounds is a careful reconstruction of Sheridan's first log cabin, erected in 1880.

The Trail End State Historic Site in Sheridan

Honor to a Hero

In 1864, the U.S. Army massacred some 300 men, women, and children in a Cheyenne village near Sand Creek, Colorado. In response, the Cheyenne and their Sioux allies attacked an army supply train on the North Platte. A twenty-one-year-old lieutenant, Caspar Collins, led a small party of soldiers to rescue the ambushed troops. All of the men with the wagon-train convoy were killed, including Collins and several soldiers from his unit. The army decided to name a fort in Collins's honor, but there was already a Fort Collins in Colorado so the fort was named Fort Caspar. No one knows for sure why the fort (and the town) later used the spelling *Casper* instead of *Caspar*. According to legend, a tired clerk made a mistake on a military report, and the change stuck. ■

Mountains and Basins

The mountain scenery of western Wyoming is among the most spectacular on Earth. The Absaroka, the Grand Teton, and the Wind River Ranges challenge the climber and backpacker and dazzle even the most casual traveler on the highway. Between the mountains are dry basins, or holes, dotted with sagebrush. Western Wyoming has few towns. Much of the land is reserved for recreation and conservation, with the Shoshone National Forest, the National Elk Refuge, Grand Teton National Park, and of course Yellowstone.

Western Wyoming Towns

At the eastern entrance to Yellowstone National Park is the town of Cody. Cody was named for one of its founders —the famous showman and Indian scout William "Buffalo Bill" Cody. The

Star of the Wild West

When he was fourteen years old, William "Buffalo Bill" Cody (1846–1917) signed on as a rider with the Pony Express. He once rode an astonishing 321 miles (517 km) in twenty-one hours, carrying bundles of letters in his horse's saddlebags. Later he killed bison to provide food for the railroad crews—and, according to some historians, to weaken the Indians by destroying their food supply. He killed 4,280 bison in one eight-month period.

Newspaper stories about Buffalo Bill's exploits made him famous. People back East were hungry for tales of Western adventure. During the 1890s, Buffalo Bill had a traveling stage show featuring gunfights, stampedes, and battles between Indians and cowboys. For a time even the famous Sioux chief Sitting Bull took part. Buffalo Bill made a fortune with his stage career, but sadly, he did not manage his money well. He died in 1917 as the real Wild West faded around him. ■

pride of this small city is the Buffalo Bill Historical Center, a complex of four exhibition halls with displays on Western history and art. The center's Buffalo Bill Museum traces the life of this legendary cowboy of the Old West. The Cody Firearms Museum contains an extensive collection of rifles from the nineteenth and early twentieth centuries. Native American crafts are on display at the Plains Indian Museum. The Whitney Gallery of Western Art has an outstanding collection of paintings and sculpture by such renowned artists as George Catlin and Frederic Remington.

The Whitney Gallery of Western Art has a remarkable collection.

The Jackson Hole region is the heart of Wyoming's ski country. Ringed with stunning mountains, the basin is dotted with resort hotels. The town of Jackson attracts many tourists. Its central square is lined with restaurants and souvenir shops, and the gates into the square are made entirely of elk horns. The National Wildlife Art Museum, located just outside Jackson, is a unique collection of work that depicts bison, elk, cougar, and other animals.

Spring Creek Resort in Jackson Hole

Blending Traditions

One of the most intriguing sites on the Wind River Reservation is St. Stephen's Mission. St. Stephen's was established as a Catholic mission to the Arapaho in the 1870s. The mission church (left), completed in 1928, combines European and Native American themes. An immense log supports the baptismal font, and the saints in the religious paintings have Indian features. ■

A Shoshone medicine man at Wind River Reservation

Shared by the Shoshone and Arapaho Indians, the Wind River Reservation covers the northern half of the Wind River Basin. Fort Washakie, used as a military outpost until 1909, now serves as reservation headquarters. Chief Washakie is buried on the reservation in a small military cemetery. A stone marks the grave of Sacajawea, though some historians do not believe that she is actually buried there.

Wyoming is dotted with ghost towns—communities that once prospered due to coal, oil, gold, or the railroad but have long since been abandoned. When gold was discovered near South Pass City in 1867, the population zoomed overnight to more than 2,000 people. But the gold quickly ran out, and the prospectors left to chase other dreams. Today South Pass City has been restored as a reminder of its bygone glory. Visitors can explore twenty-five homes and shops, a theater, a hotel, and one of the town's many saloons. Along the streets stand wagons, carriages, and even an antique manure spreader. South Pass City gives new life to Wyoming's rich and colorful past.

CHAPTER SEVEN

The Spirit of Wyoming

The capitol in Cheyenne, Wyoming, is decorated with paintings and pieces of sculpture. Perhaps the most famous of these artworks is the statue of a cowboy on a bucking horse. The cowboy seems to be getting the worst of the struggle. He has lost one stirrup and is desperately clinging to the horse's mane, but he has not fallen off. He is determined to hang on, come what may. This statue, *The Spirit of Wyoming*, is pictured on Wyoming's automobile license plates. It symbolizes the sense of adventure in which Wyomingites take pride. The people of Wyoming are tough and resilient. They hold on even when the going gets rough. The government of Wyoming, the Equality State, reflects the rugged character of the state's people.

The state capitol in Cheyenne

Opposite: Indian paintbrush, Wyoming's state flower

The Legislative Branch

On the second Tuesday in January in every odd-numbered year, the Wyoming legislature meets for a general session in the state capitol. Budgetary sessions in the legislature begin on the third Monday in February in even-numbered years. The legislature is one of the three branches of Wyoming's state government. Its purpose is to make and repeal state laws.

The legislature consists of two divisions, or houses. The upper house, or senate, has thirty members. State senators are elected to four-year terms and may serve no more than three terms during a twenty-four-year period. The house of representatives, or lower house of the legislature, has sixty members. Representatives are elected to two-year terms and may serve a total of twelve years during a twenty-four-year period.

The Judicial Branch

The judicial branch of the state government interprets the laws that are passed by the legislature. The judicial, or court, system resembles a pyramid. At the top is the state supreme court, the highest court in the state. Its five justices serve eight-year terms. Below the supreme court are nine district courts, each with one or two judges. District court judges serve six-year terms. Below the district courts are an array of police courts, municipal courts, and justice of the peace courts. There are twenty-three county courts, one for each county in the state.

The Executive Branch

The governor is the head of the executive branch of Wyoming's government. He or she is responsible for making sure that the

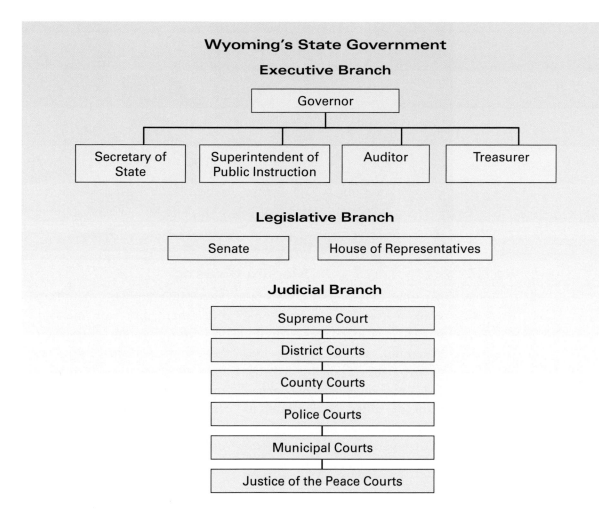

Wyoming's State Government

Executive Branch

Governor

| Secretary of State | Superintendent of Public Instruction | Auditor | Treasurer |

Legislative Branch

| Senate | House of Representatives |

Judicial Branch

Supreme Court

District Courts

County Courts

Police Courts

Municipal Courts

Justice of the Peace Courts

state laws are executed, or carried out. Many state officials are appointed by the governor, including members of the state board of education and the Wyoming Arts Council. The governor also appoints judges to the state supreme court. At the next election, the voters decide whether the appointed judge should retain his or her

Madam Governor

In 1924, Wyoming governor William Ross died suddenly of appendicitis. In the next election, Wyoming voters chose his widow, Nellie Tayloe Ross (1876–1977), to complete her husband's term of office. Trained as a kindergarten teacher, Mrs. Ross had never been interested in politics. She had not even been involved in the woman suffrage movement that won the right to vote for women nationwide. Yet she made history as the first woman governor ever inaugurated in the United States. Nellie Tayloe Ross served out her husband's term, but she was defeated in the election of 1926. ■

position. Wyoming has no lieutenant governor. If the governor cannot complete his or her term, the secretary of state takes over until the next election.

Political Wyoming

Wyoming is usually regarded as a strongly Republican state. About 54 percent of all Wyomingites are registered Republicans, and 36

Wyoming's Governors

Name	Party	Term	Name	Party	Term
Francis E. Warren	Rep.	1890	Alonzo M. Clark	Rep.	1931–1933
Amos W. Barber	Rep.	1890–1893	Leslie A. Miller	Dem.	1933–1939
John E. Osborne	Dem.	1893–1895	Nels H. Smith	Rep.	1939–1943
William A. Richards	Rep.	1895–1899	Lester C. Hunt	Dem.	1943–1949
DeForest Richards	Rep.	1899–1903	Arthur Griswold Crane	Rep.	1949–1951
Fenimore Chatterton	Rep.	1903–1905	Frank A. Barrett	Rep.	1951–1953
Bryant B. Brooks	Rep.	1905–1911	C. J. Rogers	Rep.	1953–1955
Joseph M. Carey	Dem.	1911–1915	Milward L. Simpson	Rep.	1955–1959
John B. Kendrick	Dem.	1915–1917	J. J. Hickey	Dem.	1959–1961
Frank L. Houx	Dem.	1917–1919	Jack R. Gage	Dem.	1961–1963
Robert D. Carey	Rep.	1919–1923	Clifford P. Hansen	Rep.	1963–1967
William B. Ross	Dem.	1923–1924	Stanley K. Hathaway	Rep.	1967–1975
Frank E. Lucas	Rep.	1924–1925	Edgar J. Herschler	Dem.	1975–1987
Nellie Tayloe Ross	Dem.	1925–1927	Mike Sullivan	Dem.	1987–1995
Frank C. Emerson	Rep.	1927–1931	Jim Geringer	Rep.	1995–

Wyoming's State Flag and Seal

Adopted in 1917, Wyoming's state flag shows a white bison on a blue background with a red border. Like a brand on the bison's flank is the state seal. The red border symbolizes Wyoming's Native Americans and the blood shed in the warfare between the Native Americans and the first white settlers.

At the center of Wyoming's state seal stands a woman on a pedestal, holding a banner with the words EQUAL RIGHTS. This central figure is flanked by pillars with lamps to represent the light of knowledge. The pillars are draped with banners depicting the state's leading industries: a cowboy for livestock and a miner for the mining industry. Below the central figure is a shield with an eagle and the number forty-four in Roman numerals (XLIV), a reminder that Wyoming was the forty-fourth state admitted to the Union. The shield also bears two significant dates: 1869, the year of Wyoming's first territorial legislature, and 1890, the year it became a state. ■

Wyoming's State Symbols

State mammal: Bison The bison, which once roamed the Great Plains in vast herds, is now carefully protected in Wyoming and other western states. The state's only wild herd survives in Yellowstone National Park. The bison was adopted as the state mammal on February 23, 1985.

State bird: Western meadowlark This plump brown songbird (left) is distinguished by a yellow breast with a distinctive V-shaped black marking. Its flutelike notes are heard in open fields and along roadsides. The western meadowlark, adopted as the state bird on February 5, 1927, helps the farmer by eating both weed seeds and insect pests.

State flower: Indian paintbrush The small greenish flowers of the Indian paintbrush are surrounded by colorful leaves called bracts. Depending on the species, the bracts can be red, yellow, orange, or white. Their striking colors make the plant look as though it had been dipped in a pot of paint. The Indian paintbrush was adopted as the state flower on January 31, 1917.

State tree: Great Plains cottonwood On the semiarid plains of eastern Wyoming, these graceful trees are a welcome sight. Cottonwoods (above) grow along streams and rivers and may reach a height of 100 feet (31 m). The thick, rough-edged leaves of the cottonwood make a clattering sound when the wind blows. The Great Plains cottonwood was adopted as the state tree on February 1, 1947.

State fish: Cutthroat trout The cutthroat trout, adopted as the state fish on February 18, 1987, is the only trout native to Wyoming.

State gemstone: Jade This typically green stone was adopted as the state gemstone on January 25, 1967.

Wyoming's State Song
"Wyoming"

Words by Charles E. Winter

Music by G. E. Knapp

The Wyoming state song was officially adopted on February 15, 1955.

In the far and mighty West,
Where the crimson sun seeks rest,
There's a growing splendid state that lies above
On the breast of this great land;
Where the massive Rockies stand,
There's Wyoming young and strong, the State I love!

Chorus:
Wyoming! Wyoming! Land of the sunlight clear!
Wyoming, Wyoming! Land that we hold so dear!
Wyoming, Wyoming! Precious art thou and thine!
Wyoming, Wyoming! Beloved State of mine!

In thy flowers wild and sweet,
Colors rare and perfumes meet;

There's the columbine so pure, the daisy too,
Wild the rose and red it springs,
White the button and its rings,
Thou art loyal for they're red and white and blue.

(Chorus)

Where thy peaks with crowned head,
Rising till the sky they wed,
Sit like snow queens ruling wood and stream and plain;
'Neath thy granite bases deep,
'Neath thy bosom's broadened sweep,
Lie the riches that have gained and brought thee fame.

(Chorus)

Other treasures thou dost hold,

Men and women thou dost mould;
True and earnest are the lives that thou dost raise;
Strength thy children thou dost teach,
Nature's truth thou givst to each,
Free and noble are thy workings and thy ways.

(Chorus)

In the nation's banner free
There's one star that has for me
A radiance pure and a splendor like the sun;
Mine it is, Wyoming's star,
Home it leads me, near or far;
O Wyoming! All my heart and love you've won!

(Chorus)

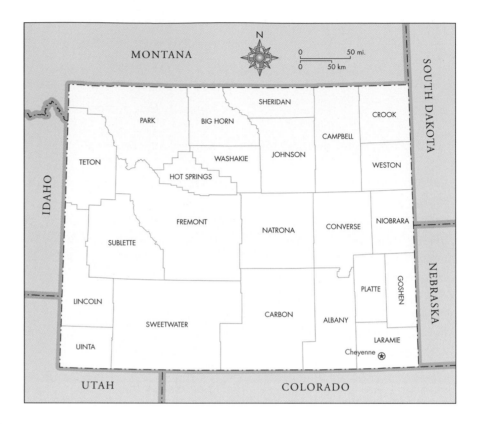

Wyoming's counties

A Voice in Washington

Wyoming Republican Alan K. Simpson (1931–) was elected to the U.S. Senate in 1978. In the early 1980s, Simpson earned national recognition as cosponsor of the Simpson-Mazzoli Bill, which sought to change U.S. policy on immigration. A revised version of the bill became law in 1986. It granted amnesty to millions of people who had entered the country illegally before 1982. From 1984 until 1987, Simpson served as majority whip, or assistant leader, in the Senate, and from 1987 to 1995, he served as minority whip. He decided not to run for reelection in 1996. ■

The War of the Wolves

During the 1980s and 1990s, Wyomingites struggled over the fate of the timber wolf, an animal once native to the state. In the early days of white settlement, ranchers and hunters killed wolves at every opportunity. By the early 1900s, wild wolves had disappeared from Wyoming. Today, however, environmentalists recognize that the wolf plays an important role in keeping elk and deer populations healthy. Environmentalists pressed the U.S. Fish and Wildlife Service to allow wolves to be reintroduced into Yellowstone National Park, and they won their case in 1995 when a number of wolves were returned to the park. Most ranchers, however, strongly oppose such legislation. They argue that wolves will soon leave the park to prey upon calves and sheep. The debate over the timber wolf has been one of the fiercest controversies in Wyoming politics. ■

percent are registered Democrats. Wyomingites tend to be suspicious of interference from "big government." This attitude is in keeping with much of the philosophy of the Republican Party.

Since the 1970s, Wyoming has consistently sent Republicans to represent the state in the U.S. Congress. In presidential elections, Wyoming has voted for Republican candidates two times out of three.

Nevertheless, the Democratic Party also has a strong foothold in Wyoming, especially in the southern half of the state. Wyoming has had many Democratic governors. Democrats are elected to other high state offices as well.

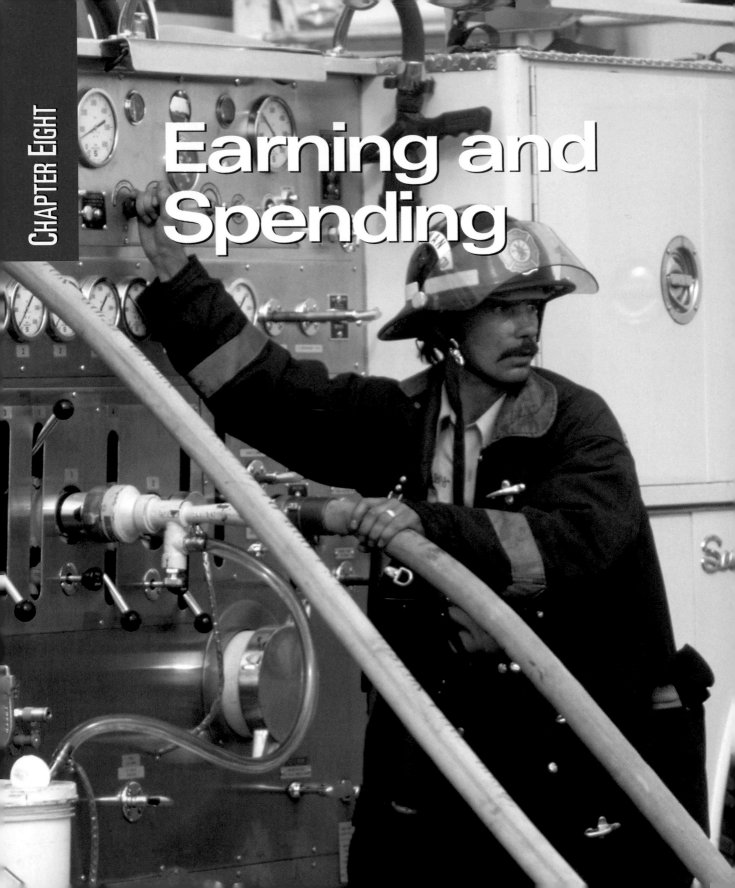

CHAPTER EIGHT

Earning and Spending

Working on an oil well south of Moneta

We don't define economic growth the way the other states do. If the alternative is high anxiety, high growth, crime, and pollution, then what we are doing is worth the gamble. When the dust settles and urbanization is complete in other states, we will be envied. Wyoming will be seen as the true New West, the last state standing with wide open spaces, clean air, and a healthy public attitude."

—Wyoming governor Jim Geringer, elected in 1994

From the Mountains and Prairies

The gross state product (GSP) is the sum total of earnings from all of a state's businesses and industries. In Wyoming, 30 percent of

Opposite: A firefighter in Cheyenne

the GSP comes from mining industries. In few other states does mining play such an important role. Wyoming is one of the leading mineral-producing states in the United States.

Ever since the first oil well gushed in 1883, petroleum has played a crucial part in Wyoming's economy. Today oil rigs operate in many parts of the state. They are especially numerous in Campbell, Park, Sweetwater, and Uinta Counties. The price of oil on the world market has a direct effect on life in Wyoming. When prices rise and oil is in demand, drilling intensifies and more people flock to the state. When prices fall, oil fields are abandoned and many of the newcomers move on again.

Because petroleum is created from the decayed remains of ancient plants and animals, it is often called a "fossil fuel." Wyoming is rich in still another fossil fuel—coal. In fact, Wyoming is the leading coal producer in the United States. In 1995, 25 percent of all U.S. coal came from the Equality State. Coal deposits are found beneath about 40 percent of Wyoming's land. The heart of Wyoming's coal country is the northeastern and south-central part of the state. The Black Thunder Mine in the Powder River Basin is the biggest coal mine in the country.

What Wyoming Grows, Manufactures, and Mines

Agriculture	Manufacturing	Mining
Beef cattle	Chemicals	Coal
Hay	Petroleum products	Natural gas
Sugar beets		Petroleum

A Wealth of Trona

Trona is a gray or yellowish crystalline mineral composed of sodium, carbon, and water. It is found in the most arid regions of the planet such as parts of Egypt and Iran. The largest deposit of trona in the United States lies deep underground near Green River, Wyoming. Mining began here in 1947. Trona is used in the production of soda ash, a compound important in the manufacture of glass, soap, and paper. ■

Another fossil fuel found in Wyoming is natural gas. Natural gas is often released from below the earth's crust during oil drilling. Most natural gas is produced in the southwestern part of the state.

In addition to fossil fuels, Wyoming yields many valuable minerals. Uranium, a radioactive element vital in the production of nuclear energy, lies in rocks in the Powder, Shirley, and Wind

River Basins. Agate and jade, both semiprecious stones, are also found in Wyoming, as are small deposits of gold. Bentonite clay, which is used in the oil-drilling process, is mined in the north-central and northwestern portions of the state.

Only 4 percent of Wyoming's GSP comes from manufacturing. This figure places Wyoming at the bottom of the list of states in terms of the value and quantity of its manufactured products. Manufactured goods from the state include chemicals (especially soda ash) and petroleum products.

Though farms and ranches occupy nearly half of Wyoming's land, agriculture accounts for only 4 percent of the state's GSP. About 80 percent of the farming in Wyoming consists of livestock production. Cattle graze on the eastern plains as they have since the 1880s. The sheep-raising industry is also important in Wyoming.

Some 20 percent of Wyoming's agricultural output comes from crops. Wyoming farmers raise sugar beets, hay, barley, wheat, beans, and corn.

Serving the Public

About 59 percent of Wyoming's GSP comes from service industries. People in service industries do not produce goods that can be
sold. Instead, they perform work that serves the public. Sales-
clerks, airline pilots, dentists, travel agents, teachers, and librarians
all work in service industries.

**Most of the state's
farming involves
raising livestock.**

Farming without Rain

Wyoming's scarce rainfall is a serious challenge to the farmer. Some farmers on the eastern plains irrigate their crops with water from the North Platte and other rivers. But many farmers practice "dry farming," using methods that allow them to raise crops without irrigation. Dry-farming techniques help the soil absorb and retain as much water as possible. Some fields may be left fallow, or unplanted, for a year to let the moisture in the soil build up again. Sometimes the stubble from harvested crops is not cleared away in the fall. It is spread on the ground during winter to help keep water in the soil from evaporating. ■

Chuck Wagon Stew

This substantial meal was a staple for cowboys and settlers of the West.

Ingredients:

- 2½ pounds beef
- 2 tablespoons flour
- 1 tablespoon paprika
- 1 teaspoon chili powder and an additional 3 tablespoons of chili powder
- 2 teaspoons salt
- 3 tablespoons shortening
- 2 onions, sliced
- 1 clove garlic, minced
- 28 ounces of tomatoes, fresh or canned
- 1 tablespoon cinnamon
- 1 teaspoon cloves, ground
- ½ teaspoon dry red peppers, crushed
- 2 cups carrots, chopped
- 2 cups potatoes, chopped

Directions:

Cut the beef into cubes, to make approximately 5 cups. In a separate bowl, mix the flour, paprika, 1 teaspoon of chili powder, and salt. Roll the beef in the mixture.

In a Dutch oven, brown the beef in the hot shortening. Add the onion and garlic, cook until soft. Blend in tomatoes, 3 tablespoons of chili powder, cinnamon, cloves, and red peppers. Cover and simmer for 2 hours.

Add carrots and potatoes. Cook for 45 minutes or until vegetables are done.

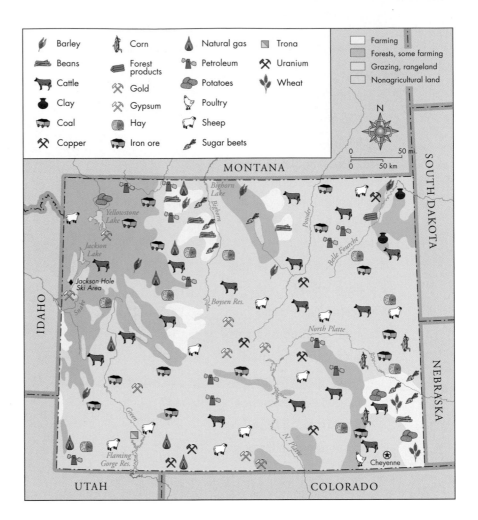

Wyoming's natural resources

Wyoming's leading service industries are those centered on transportation, communication, and utilities. This broad field includes everything from power plants and oil pipelines to cable TV stations. Finance, insurance, and real estate comprise the second-largest service category in the state. These services are most heavily concentrated in Casper and Cheyenne.

Do unto Others

As a teenager, James Cash Penney (1875–1971) went to work in a general store in Hamilton, Wyoming. In 1902, he and a partner opened a store of their own in Kemmerer. Within a few years, Penney had established a chain of stores around the United States. They were called Golden Rule Stores in the early days, but the name was later changed to J. C. Penney.

Penney retired in 1946, determined to use his wealth for the good of humanity. His J. C. Penney Foundation supports projects in the fields of religion, science, and education. ■

The federal government is the biggest single employer in the state of Wyoming. The government owns and manages about half of the state's land. It controls logging, grazing, and water use, as well as hunting and fishing. It also maintains the state's national forests, national monuments, and national parks. The federal government also operates Warren Air Force Base.

Each year, visitors to Wyoming spend about $1.5 billion. Tourism is big business in Wyoming. National parks, ski resorts, and the state's Wild West mystique lure people from all over the world. Tourism creates jobs in hotels, visitors' centers, parks, and shops of all kinds.

Reaching Out to the World

In the late 1800s, the Union Pacific Railroad spurred the development of many of Wyoming's cities and towns. Passenger trains no longer serve the state, though Wyoming still has three freight lines. Today most people travel within the state by truck or automobile.

Traveling along a Wyoming road

Wyoming has 39,000 miles (62,750 km) of paved roads and highways. The state's busiest airport is in Jackson, which serves the ski areas of Jackson Hole.

The first newspaper in Wyoming was the *Daily Telegraph*, published at Fort Bridger in 1863. Today Wyoming has eight daily papers, including the *Casper Star-Tribune* and Cheyenne's *Wyoming Tribune-Eagle*.

A Man and His Mule

In 1881, a former railroad man named Bill Nye (right) began to publish a newspaper in Laramie, Wyoming. He named his paper the *Boomerang* after his trusty mule. Nye's columns crackled with irreverent humor. He is sometimes compared to America's greatest satirist, Mark Twain. After publishing his wit in Laramie for six years, Nye left for New York City. There, he won fame and fortune as a popular columnist with the *New York World*. ■

Wyoming was one of the last states to launch a radio station. KDFN (now KTWO) began broadcasting from Casper in 1930, nearly a decade after radio was established in more populous states. Television came to Wyoming in 1954, when KFBC-TV (now KGWN) went on the air in Cheyenne. Today Wyoming has thirteen TV stations, two cable-TV systems, and about fifty-five radio stations.

CHAPTER NINE

Old Timers and the New Breed

This area is beginning to change very rapidly. People are moving here who weren't raised here. They have different ideas on how to care for the national forests, and I believe the cattle industry will be precluded. The era I grew up in is rapidly approaching its close. I can change my business and stay in the same place, or change places and stay in the same business."

—Wyoming rancher Don Tolman

Wyoming is home to old timers and newcomers.

Off the Beaten Track

In this day of high-speed travel and instant communication, Wyoming is no longer a remote frontier outpost. Yet the lifestyle and mind-set of longtime Wyoming families often differ from

Opposite: A cowboy from Casper

Population of Wyoming's Major Cities (1990)

City	Population
Cheyenne	50,008
Casper	46,742
Laramie	26,687
Rock Springs	19,050
Gillette	17,635
Sheridan	13,900

Wyoming's population density

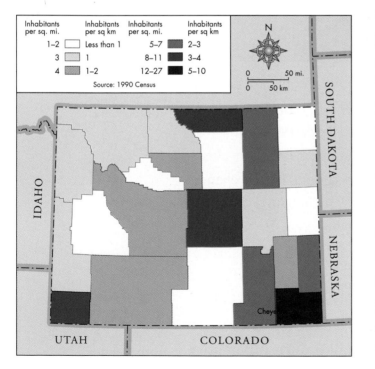

those of people in more densely settled parts of the United States. Wyomingites love the land from which they make their living. They are resentful when newcomers try to make rules about how the land should be put to use. Nevertheless, the influx of newcomers brings many benefits to the state. As more people flock to Wyoming, the economy improves.

Tensions mounted between old and new ways during the population boom of the 1970s. Between 1970 and 1980, Wyoming's population increased by 42 percent. No other state saw such a dramatic upsurge. Most of this sudden growth was spurred by increased demand for Wyoming's oil. Thousands of people moved to the state to work in the petroleum industry. Wyoming's population growth slowed somewhat during the 1980s and 1990s. Yet more and more outsiders—generally people from urban areas—are still drawn to the state each year. Wyoming's population rose from 332,000 in 1970 to 479,743, according to government estimates, in 1997.

Despite this rapid growth, Wyoming ranks fiftieth in population among the states. The entire state has about the same number of residents as New Orleans, Louisiana. On average, Wyoming has only 5 persons per square mile (2 per sq km). However, this does not mean that most Wyomingites live in wide-open spaces. The population is heavily concentrated along the highways and railway lines in the southern part of the state. About 65 percent of all Wyomingites are classified as urban dwellers. According to population experts, urban dwellers are persons who live in towns or cities of 2,500 people or more.

The biggest city in Wyoming is the state capital, Cheyenne, with about 50,000 people. Cheyenne is followed by Casper with almost 47,000 and Laramie with nearly 27,000. Other cities of more than 10,000 people include Rock Springs, Gillette, and Sheridan. Casper and Cheyenne have the state's only metropolitan areas.

Downtown Cheyenne

Who Are the Wyomingites?

The vast majority of Wyoming's people—94 percent—are of European ancestry. Most of their forebears came from Great Britain, Germany, or Ireland. Wyoming has very few immigrants from other countries. About 98 percent of all Wyomingites were born in the United States.

Nevertheless, nearly every ethnic group is represented in Wyoming. Spanish is the first language of about 13,000 Wyomingites. Most of these Spanish-speaking

Four generations of Arapaho women

Room for the Second Son

In nineteenth-century England, firstborn sons inherited most of their fathers' money and land. The second son of the family received only a small stipend by comparison. Many of these second sons took what money they had and immigrated to Wyoming. There they purchased land and went into the ranching business. Some of the leading ranchers in the state were the sons and grandsons of English lords. When Queen Elizabeth II visited the state, she called on some of these Wyoming aristocrats.

people are of Mexican descent. Some 9,000 people in the state are classified as Native Americans. The largest Indian group is the Arapaho, followed by the Shoshone. Some 1,600 of Wyoming's Indians still speak their native languages fluently. Wyoming also has small populations of Asians and African-Americans.

Roman Catholics comprise the single largest religious group in Wyoming. About 60,000 Wyomingites belong to the Roman Catholic Church. Another 45,000 people in the state are practicing Mormons, members of the Church of Jesus Christ of Latter-day Saints. Other Christian denominations in the state include Methodist, Episcopalian, Southern Baptist, and Lutheran.

Shepherds of the Mountains

Many of Wyoming's sheep ranchers are the descendants of Basque shepherds who moved to the region in the late 1800s. The Basques are native to the Pyrenees Mountains of Spain, where they have a long tradition of herding sheep and goats. They have their own language, their own unique customs, and their own legends. In the semiarid mountains of Wyoming, the Basques felt they had found a familiar landscape.

Going to School

In 1852, William Vaux, the chaplain at Fort Laramie, began to teach reading and writing to a handful of children who lived at the post. Vaux's school was the first in the territory. A similar school was established in 1860 at Fort Bridger. In 1869, the territorial legisla-

ture passed a law that provided tax support for public education. The territory's first high school opened in Cheyenne in 1875.

Today, law requires all Wyoming children to attend school between the ages of seven and fifteen, or until graduation from eighth grade. Wyoming has one of the highest literacy rates in the United States.

About half of all adult Wyomingites are college graduates. Wyoming has one private college and eight public institutions of higher learning, including the University of Wyoming at Laramie.

Wyoming students at a country school

CHAPTER TEN

Celebrating the West

A rodeo at Cheyenne
Frontier Days

Each July, thousands of people pour into Cheyenne for the annual extravaganza known as Cheyenne Frontier Days. This rollicking festival dates back to 1897. For ten days the city becomes the backdrop for a glorious series of rodeos, parades, and country-music concerts. Native Americans from the Wind River Reservation and other reservations set up a tepee village, demonstrate Indian crafts, and perform traditional dances. Cooks prepare cowboy-style meals on vintage chuck wagons, using antique pots and ladles. Craftspeople exhibit tooled leather belts, pine furniture, and even doorknobs made of rattlesnake rattles.

Cheyenne Frontier Days is a lively celebration of Western history and the Wyoming way of life. This Western theme plays through Wyoming's arts and literature. And of course the Western

Opposite: Riding in
Shoshone National
Forest

setting shapes the ways in which Wyomingites enjoy sports and outdoor recreation.

Picturing Wyoming

In 1872, an expedition led by Ferdinand Hayden ventured into the wilderness of northwestern Wyoming. Among the explorers were a painter named Thomas Moran and a photographer, William Henry Jackson. With their brushes and cameras, these two artists captured the splendor of the mountains and canyons, and the star-

Names on the Landscape

In Grand Teton National Park, Lake Jackson lies at the foot of Mount Moran. William Henry Jackson took the first photographs of Lake Jackson in 1877, but the lake is not named after him. It is actually named for David Jackson, an early trapper and explorer in the American West. Mount Moran is named in honor of the painter Thomas Moran, but Moran never laid eyes on the mountain that now bears his name. ■

tling beauty of forests, geysers, and paint pots. Their pictures helped persuade Congress to set the Yellowstone region aside as the world's first national park.

Moran and Jackson were not the first artists to find inspiration in Wyoming. George Catlin (1796–1872) traveled the Great Plains and Rocky Mountain regions between 1829 and 1836. Catlin was fascinated by the Native Americans of the West and tried to capture their way of life in his sketches and paintings. In 1845, he published an illustrated book called *Catlin's*. Catlin is best known for his illustrated two-volume work *Letters and Notes on the Manners, Customs, and Conditions of the North American Indians* (1841).

In 1863, a German-born painter named Albert Bierstadt (1830–1902) made the first of several journeys into the Rockies. On these expeditions, Bierstadt filled his sketchpads with landscape drawings. When he returned to his studio in New York, he transformed his sketches into magnificent paintings of sweeping mountain panoramas. Bierstadt's work became immensely popular and helped the West gain a special place in the American imagination.

Painter Albert Bierstadt is known for his landscapes of the American West.

While Bierstadt painted landscapes, Frederic Remington (1861–1909) was intrigued with the action and drama of the

The Herd at Night by
Frederic Remington

West. Born in Upstate New York, Remington traveled widely on the Great Plains and in the Rocky Mountains. His paintings depict Indians, cowhands, and frontier battles. He also created beautifully detailed bronze sculptures of galloping horses, stampeding cattle, and other Western scenes. The Whitney Gallery of Western Art at the Buffalo Bill Museum in Cody has an extensive collection of Remington's work. The museum also has a reconstruction of the studio where he did most of his painting.

Frederic Remington created sculptures and paintings that depict Western scenes.

Wild Moments

One of the most unusual art museums in the United States is the National Museum of Wildlife Art, which opened north of Jackson in 1997. The museum's twelve galleries are alive with paintings and sculptures of wild animals in their natural habitats. One gallery is devoted to depictions of bison. One of the artists whose work is on display is Charles M. Russell (1864–1926). Russell traveled throughout the West, especially in Montana and Wyoming. As a young man herding cattle, he always carried a lump of soft wax in his pocket. While he sat by the campfire he would shape the wax into a bear, a cougar, or some other creature he had observed on his wanderings. Later he made larger animal figures with clay. Russell's work is remarkable for its attention to detail. He studied the bodies of animals killed by hunters in order to learn the correct anatomy. ■

Painter without a Brush

One of Wyoming's most famous native sons, Jackson Pollock (1912–1956) was among the leading American artists of the twentieth century. He was born in Cody but left the West in 1929 to study painting in New York. During the 1940s, Pollock began to drip paint over his canvas from sticks and even to pour the paint directly from a can. With these innovative techniques, he created complex patterns of color and texture. Pollock is considered the founder of the school of art known as abstract expressionism. He died in an automobile accident when he was only forty-four years old. ∎

Western themes still pervade the work of Wyoming artists. Many painters live in and around the scenic town of Jackson, where their work is displayed in galleries year-round and on the streets in summer art fairs. Some of these paintings explore the possibilities of abstract modern art. But many others are scenes of horses, cowboys, and the vast, open country that is Wyoming.

Telling the Story

The writer Washington Irving (1783–1859) is the author of such American classics as "Rip Van Winkle" and "The Legend of Sleepy Hollow." These tales are based on legends from New York's Hudson River valley. Few people realize that Irving helped to preserve some of the tales of early Wyoming as well. Irving traveled west just once in 1832, but John Jacob Astor commissioned him to write a history of his powerful American Fur Company. In 1836, Irving published *Astoria: or, Anecdotes of an Enterprise beyond the Rocky Mountains*. Irving's history draws upon the letters and journals of many white fur traders who explored Wyoming in the 1820s and 1830s.

Stories in Song

Sometimes a real-life event inspires someone to write a ballad—a story in the form of a song. One such ballad praised the heroism of Nick Ray and Nate Champion, Wyoming cowboys who were killed during the Johnson County War of 1892. While held under siege in a cabin near Kaycee, Champion wrote his thoughts in a journal. Champion's journal was the basis for the ballad, which helped rally small ranchers against the cattle barons:

It was a little blood-stained book
Which a bullet had torn in twain,
It told the fate of Nick and Nate
Which is known to all of you.
He had the nerve to write it down
While bullets fell like rain,
At your request I'll do my best
To read these lines again. . .

The light is out, the curtain's drawn,
The last sad act is played.
You know the fate that met poor Nate,
And of the run he made.
But now across the Big Divide
And at the home ranch door,
I know he'll meet and warmly greet
The boys that went before.

During the years when Wyoming was a territory, few residents had time to write books about their experiences. But Wyomingites loved to tell stories. After a long day on the trail, cowboys gathered around the campfire. They talked about encounters with wolves and grizzly bears, run-ins with rustlers, and other adventures. Their stories often grew wilder and more fantastic with each retelling.

The life and lore of the cowboy gave rise to a new form of American literature called the Western. One of the first and most influential Western novels was *The Virginian* (1902) by Owen Wister (1860–1938). Wister grew up in Philadelphia, studied music in Europe, and earned a law degree from Harvard. In 1885, he spent the first of several summers in Wyoming. Much of *The Virginian* is set in the town of Medicine Bow. *The Virginian* became a longtime best-seller, a Broadway play, and a Hollywood movie. It even inspired a TV series in the 1960s.

Two Wyoming authors wrote for both adult and younger readers. Will James described ranch life in such books as *Cowboys North and South* (1924), *Cow Country* (1927), and *All in a Day's Riding* (1933). His 1926 children's book, *Smoky the Cowhorse*, is considered a classic. Like Will James, Mary O'Hara is best known for her popular children's books about horses. Her novel *My Friend Flicka* (1941) was the basis for a tele-

The cast from *The Virginian* television show

Owen Wister Remembered

Outside the town of Medicine Bow stands a stone pyramid erected in 1939 in honor of novelist Owen Wister. Downtown, the Virginian Hotel is on the National Register of Historic Places. Its rooms are furnished in the style that was popular around 1902, when *The Virginian* was published.

Medicine Bow treats Owen Wister with the greatest respect. Wister was far less kind to Medicine Bow, however. In *The Virginian* he described it by saying: "Until our language stretches itself and takes in a word of a closer fit, 'town' will have to do. I have seen and slept in many like it since—stark, dotted over a planet of treeless dust, like soiled packs of cards. . . . They seemed to have been strewn here by the wind, and to be waiting till the wind should come again and blow them away." ∎

vision series in the 1950s. In *Wyoming Summer* (1961), O'Hara describes day-to-day life on her ranch near Laramie.

Author Mary O'Hara is best known for writing *My Friend Flicka*.

Gathering Together

During the 1830s, Wyoming mountain men gathered once a year for their annual rendezvous. The rendezvous was far more than a business meeting where trappers sold their furs. It was a gala party, a time of feasting, games, and storytelling that brought everyone together. Wyomingites are no longer as lonely and isolated as those early mountain men. But they still enjoy getting together for music, theater, and outdoor recreation.

The Mountain Men Rendezvous at Teton Village outside Jackson is a fun-filled reminder of the rendezvous of old. Each year over Memorial Day weekend, history buffs dress in buckskin, camp in tents, and cook over open fires. On this special weekend they live as the mountain men lived long ago. The highlight of the ren-

Teton Village's Mountain Men Rendezvous

dezvous is a staged shoot-out, a humorous skit that pits good guys against bad guys. The shooting is done with black-powder rifles, the firearms widely used in the 1830s and 1840s.

The Mountain Men Rendezvous coincides with Old West Days, a festival that brings some 20,000 people to Jackson each year. This four-day festival features music, parades, rodeos, and traditional Native American dancing by the Fort Hall Dancers from Idaho.

Jackson hosts a very different festival each September. The Jackson Hole Fall Arts Festival is a ten-day celebration of the fine arts. Some thirty galleries host special exhibits by local artists and others from across the nation. For one delightful event, Pinkie Painting on the Square, children and adults are invited to experiment with fingerpainting. Their uninhibited creations are put on public display. The fall arts festival leads straight into a three-week festival called Arts for the Parks, featuring paintings, drawings, and sculptures inspired by national parks throughout the United States.

Wyoming winters are perfect for skiing.

The Grand Teton Music Festival is held for two months each summer. The festival offers music lovers a delectable menu of symphonies, chamber music, and solo performances. Many concerts feature the Casper-based Wyoming Symphony Orchestra. Other well-known groups from around the country also appear regularly.

Outdoor Fun

Wyomingites love all forms of outdoor recreation. Winter brings snow for skiing, snowshoeing, and tobogganing. Summer days are filled with fishing, hiking, and mountain climbing. In the fall, hunters stalk deer, antelope, and elk. Nearly every Wyoming family owns a tent, sleeping bags, and other camping gear.

A favorite sport in Wyoming is the rodeo, which became popular late in the nineteenth century. The rodeo began as a means for cowhands to show off their skills in roping and riding. It has evolved into a colorful spectacle in which professional riders put on a magnificent performance and compete for big cash prizes. A rodeo involves two kinds of events: rough stock events and timed events. In rough stock events, men or women attempt to ride bulls or bucking broncos. In timed events, the contestants must rope calves or steers, ride through an

The rodeo is one of Wyoming's favorite entertainments.

A Chance to Play Cowboy

In 1904, a Wyoming rancher named Howard Eaton invited several friends from back East for an extended visit. The easterners were thrilled with the chance to ride horses, rope cattle, and help at branding time. Over the following years, Eaton opened his ranch to paying guests. The Eaton Ranch is the oldest of Wyoming's many "dude ranches." At most dude ranches, visitors may spend two weeks or more getting a taste of cowboy life. For people of all ages, dude ranches provide activities such as trail rides, storytelling, and cooking over an open fire. Some even surprise their guests with a staged hold-up featuring gunslingers in black hats. ■

Fallen Hero

At the entrance to the Cheyenne Frontier Days Old West Museum is a statue of a young man clinging to the back of a bucking bull. The statue represents Lane Frost, one of the finest bull riders in the United States, who was killed during a Frontier Days rodeo in 1989. Among rodeo fans, Lane Frost is honored as a hero and a legend. ■

obstacle course, or perform some other feat within a given number of seconds. Between these events, most rodeos have clown acts and band shows.

The most spectacular rodeo series in Wyoming, and one of the best in the nation, can be seen during Cheyenne Frontier Days. A rodeo is held every afternoon throughout the ten-day festival. The Frontier Days rodeos draw top contestants from as far away as Australia.

The first time you see a rider struggling with a bucking horse at a Wyoming rodeo, you may have the feeling you have glimpsed the scene before. Perhaps you are remembering the famous statue at the Wyoming capitol in Cheyenne. Perhaps you are thinking of the emblem on the Wyoming license plate. To the people of the Equality State, the daring rider on the back of the lunging horse is an undying symbol. It is the spirit of Wyoming.

Timeline

United States History

The first permanent English settlement is established in North America at Jamestown. **1607**

Pilgrims found Plymouth Colony, the second permanent English settlement. **1620**

America declares its independence from Britain. **1776**

The Treaty of Paris officially ends the Revolutionary War in America. **1783**

The U.S. Constitution is written. **1787**

The Louisiana Purchase almost doubles the size of the United States. **1803**

The United States and Britain **1812–15** fight the War of 1812.

The North and South fight **1861–65** each other in the American Civil War.

Wyoming State History

1742 François and Louis-Joseph La Vérendrye are the first Europeans to enter Wyoming.

1807 John Colter explores the Yellowstone area.

1812 Robert Stuart discovers the South Pass through the Rocky Mountains.

1834 John Sublette and Robert Campbell establish a trading post on the Laramie and North Platte Rivers.

1843 Jim Bridger establishes Fort Bridger.

1867 The Union Pacific Railroad enters Wyoming.

1868 The U.S. Congress creates the Wyoming Territory.

United States History

The United States is **1917–18**
involved in World War I.

The stock market crashes, **1929**
plunging the United States into
the Great Depression.

The United States **1941–45**
fights in World War II.
The United States becomes a **1945**
charter member of the U.N.

The United States **1951–53**
fights in the Korean War.

The U.S. Congress enacts a series of **1964**
groundbreaking civil rights laws.

The United States **1964–73**
engages in the Vietnam War.

The United States and other **1991**
nations fight the brief
Persian Gulf War against Iraq.

Wyoming State History

1869 The Wyoming territorial legislature
gives women the right to vote and hold
office.

1872 Yellowstone becomes the first national
park in the United States.

1890 Wyoming becomes the 44th state on
July 10.

1900–10 Bloody skirmishes occur between
cattle ranchers and sheep raisers.

1906 President Theodore Roosevelt makes
Devils Tower the first national monument in the United States.

1925 Nellie Tayloe Ross becomes the first
woman governor in the United States.

1951–52 Major uranium deposits are
found in several parts of the state.

1960 The first intercontinental ballistic missile base opens near Cheyenne.

1965 Minuteman missile installations are
completed near Cheyenne.

1988 Fires damage large areas of
Yellowstone National Park.

Fast Facts

State capitol

Statehood date July 10, 1890; the 44th state

Origin of state name In the language of the Leni-Lenape, Indians of eastern Pennsylvania, *Wyoming* means "on the plains." It was first suggested by a congressman from Ohio in 1865.

State capital Cheyenne

State nickname Equality State

State motto "Equal Rights"

State bird Western meadowlark

State fish Cutthroat trout

Great Plains
cottonwood

Fishing in the
Snake River

State flower	Indian paintbrush
State mammal	Bison
State gemstone	Jade
State fossil	Knightia
State dinosaur	Triceratops
State reptile	Horned toad
State song	"Wyoming"
State tree	Great Plains cottonwood
State fair	Late August in Douglas
Total area; rank	97,819 sq. mi. (253,351 sq km); 9th
Land; rank	97,105 sq. mi. (251,502 sq km); 9th
Water; rank	714 sq. mi. (1,849 sq km); 35th
***Inland water;* rank**	714 sq. mi. (1,849 sq km); 30th
Geographic center	Fremont, 58 miles (93 km) northeast of Lander
Latitude and longitude	Wyoming is located approximately between 104° 03' and 111° 03' W and 41° 45' N
Highest point	Gannett Peak, 13,804 feet (4,210 m)
Lowest point	3,099 feet (945 m) at Belle Fourche River
Largest city	Cheyenne
Number of counties	23
Population; rank	455,975 (1990 census); 50th
Density	5 persons per sq. mi. (2 per sq km)

Arapaho women

Population distribution	65% urban, 35% rural	
Ethnic distribution (does not equal 100%)	White	94.15%
	Hispanic	5.69%
	Other	2.34%
	Native American	2.09%
	African-American	0.79%
	Asian and Pacific Islanders	0.62%

Record high temperature	114°F (46°C) at Basin on July 12, 1900
Record low temperature	–63°F (–53°C) at Moran, near Elk, on February 9, 1933
Average July temperature	67°F (19°C)
Average January temperature	19°F (–7°C)
Average annual precipitation	13 inches (33 cm)

Grand Teton National Park

Natural Areas and Historic Site

National Parks

Grand Teton National Park encompasses the most impressive peaks of the Teton Range as well as Jackson Hole.

Yellowstone National Park, the first national park in the United States, contains one of the finest geyser fields in the world. Parts of the park are also in Montana and Idaho.

Devils Tower

National Recreation Area
Bighorn Canyon National Recreation Area contains Bighorn Lake, which was formed by the building of the Yellowtail Dam on the Bighorn River in 1966. Parts of the recreation area are also in Montana.

National Monuments
Devils Tower National Monument is a volcanic tower that rises 867 feet (264 m) above its base.

Fossil Butte National Monument protects the fossil remains of freshwater fish as well as insects, birds, and plants.

National Historic Site
Fort Laramie National Historic Site preserves the remains of the military fort that protected wagon trains traveling west from 1849 to 1890.

National Parkway
John D. Rockefeller Jr. Memorial Parkway is a scenic area dedicated to the memory of the man responsible for the preservation of many natural areas.

A forest of lodgepole pines

National Forests
Bighorn National Forest, established in 1897, contains 1.1 million acres (445,500 ha) within an area roughly 80 miles (129 km) long and 30 miles (48 km) wide. Cloud Peak Wilderness within its boundaries preserves the highest peak in the Bighorn Mountains.

Black Hills National Forest covers 175,000 acres (70,875 ha) in Wyoming and another 1 million acres (405,000 ha) in South Dakota. The Lakota Sioux called these hills "Paha Sapa," or "hills that are black," because the ponderosa pine slopes are dark when seen from the plains.

Shoshone National Forest

Bridger-Teton National Forest is the second largest national forest outside Alaska, covering more than 3.4 million acres (1,377,000 ha). The Teton Wilderness is south of Yellowstone National Park and home to grizzly bears and great hunting and fishing. The Bridger Wilderness, on the west slope of the Wind River Range north and east of Pinedale, is a favorite of backpackers. The Gros Ventre Wilderness is a mountainous area located east of Jackson.

Medicine Bow National Forest covers more than 1 million acres (405,000 ha) in southeastern Wyoming, as well as the Thunder Basin National Grassland in northeast Wyoming.

Shoshone National Forest is more than 2.4 million acres (972,000 ha) of outstanding scenery and wildlife. It contains five wildernesses areas: Washakie Wilderness, Absaroka-Beartooth and North Absaroka Wilderness, Popo Agie Wilderness, and Fitzpatrick Wilderness.

Targhee National Forest lies primarily in Idaho but has two wildernesses within Wyoming. The Jedediah Smith Wilderness is located on the west slope of the Teton Range, and the smaller Winegar Hole Wilderness lies next to the southwest corner of Yellowstone National Park.

State Parks
Wyoming maintains twenty-two state parks and historic sites, the largest of which is Boysen State Park in central Wyoming.

Cultural Institutions

Libraries
The William Robertson Coe Library at the University of Wyoming at Laramie is the state's largest library.

The State Library of Wyoming (Cheyenne), the state's second-largest library, houses a valuable collection of law literature. This library was established in 1871 as the Wyoming Territorial Library.

University of Wyoming

Museums
Wyoming State Museum (Cheyenne) contains fine exhibits about pioneer days and Native American heritage.

Cheyenne Frontier Days Old West Museum also features collections about pioneer life and Native American history.

Buffalo Bill Historical Center (Cody) commemorates the life and preserves the belongings of the famous hunter and Wild West showman.

The University of Wyoming Geological Museum (Laramie) displays fine collections on natural history including fossils, minerals, and rocks as well as exhibits about prehistoric times.

Universities and Colleges
In the late 1990s, Wyoming had eight public institutions of higher learning and one private institution of higher learning.

Sports Teams

NCAA Teams (Division 1)
University of Wyoming Cowboys

Annual Events

January–March
Wyoming State Winter Fair in Lander (January)

Cutter races near Afton, Big Piney, Jackson, Pinedale, and Saratoga (February)

April–June
Woodchopper's Jamboree Encampment (mid-June)

Chugwater Chili Cookoff in Chugwater (July)

July–September
Pioneer Days in Lander (July 1–4)

Jubilee Days in Laramie (first week in July)

Roping at a rodeo

Central Wyoming Fair in Casper (mid-July)

Indian Sun Dances in Ethete and Fort Washakie (late July)

Cheyenne Frontier Days in Cheyenne (July)

Cody Stampede Rodeo in Cody (July)

Green River Rendezvous near Pinedale (July)

Sheridan Rodeo in Sheridan (July)

Indian Pageant in Thermopolis (early August)

State Fair in Douglas (late August)

Cowboy Days Rodeo in Evanston (Labor Day)

Fort Bridger Rendezvous in Fort Bridger (Labor Day)

Jackson Hole Arts Festival in Jackson Hole (September)

Famous People

Butch Cassidy

James Bridger (1804–1881)	Frontiersman, fur trader, and scout
Martha Jane "Calamity Jane" Cannary Burk (1852–1903)	Frontierswoman
Butch Cassidy (1866–1908)	Outlaw
George Catlin (1796–1872)	Artist
William Frederick "Buffalo Bill" Cody (1846–1917)	Frontiersman and entertainer
John Colter (1775?–1813)	Fur trader
Crazy Horse (1844–1877)	Indian leader
Gretel Ehrlich (1964–)	Author
Emerson Hough (1857–1923)	Author
Thomas Moran (1837–1923)	Artist
Esther Morris (1814–1902)	Judge
Edgar Wilson (Bill) Nye (1850–1896)	Humorist

Mary O'Hara (1885–1980)   Author
James Cash Penney (1875–1971)   Businessman
Jackson Pollock (1912–1956)   Artist
Red Cloud (1822–1909)   Indian leader
Nellie Tayloe Ross (1876–1977)   Public official
Charles M. Russell (1864–1926)   Artist
Alan K. Simpson (1931–)   Politician
Washakie (1804–1900)   Indian leader
Owen Wister (1860–1938)   Author

Owen Wister

To Find Out More

History

- Fradin, Dennis Brindell. *Wyoming*. Chicago: Childrens Press, 1994.

- Frisch, Carlienne. *Wyoming*. Minneapolis: Lerner, 1994.

- Thompson, Kathleen. *Wyoming*. Austin, Tex.: Raintree/Steck Vaughn, 1996.

Fiction

- George, Jean Craighead. *One Day in the Alpine Tundra*. New York: Harper-Collins Children's Books, 1984.

- O'Hara. Mary. *My Friend Flicka*. New York: Harper-Collins Juvenile Books, 1988.

- Paulsen, Gary. *The Haymeadow*. New York: Delacorte Press, 1992.

- Wallace, Bill. *Red Dog*. New York: Holiday House, 1987.

Biographies

- Faber, Doris. *Calamity Jane: Her Life and Her Legend*. New York: Houghton Mifflin, 1992.

- Venezia, Mike. *Jackson Pollock*. Chicago: Childrens Press, 1994.

Websites

- **Wyoming State Website**
  http://www.state.wy.us/state/welcome.html
  The official state website

- **Yellowstone National Park**
  http://www.nps.gov/yell/home.htm
  A cybertour of the nation's oldest national park

Addresses

- **Wyoming Division of Tourism**
  I-25 and College Drive
  Cheyenne, WY 82002
  For information about travel and tourism in Wyoming

- **Wyoming Division of Economic and Community Development**
  Barrett Building
  Cheyenne, WY 82002
  For information about Wyoming's economy

- **Wyoming Legislative Service Office**
  Capitol
  Cheyenne, WY 82002
  For information about Wyoming's government

- **Wyoming Historical and Archaeological Resources**
  Barrett Building
  Cheyenne, WY 82002
  For information about Wyoming's history

Index

Page numbers in *italics* indicate illustrations.

Meet the Author

Deborah Kent grew up in Little Falls, New Jersey. She received a bachelor's degree in English from Oberlin College and a master's degree from Smith College School for Social Work. On completing her studies, she worked at the University Settlement House on New York's Lower East Side.

After four years at the settlement house, Ms. Kent decided to pursue her lifelong interest in writing. She moved to San Miguel de Allende, a town in the mountains of Mexico, which had a lively colony of writers and artists. In San Miguel, she wrote her first book, a young-adult novel called *Belonging*. Since then she has published fifteen young-adult novels and more than forty nonfiction titles for young readers.

While writing *Wyoming*, Ms. Kent became fascinated by the history and natural wonders of the state. She loved talking to

Wyomingites about their interests and their way of life. One enthusiastic source of first-hand information was her cousin, Grant Linck, a University of Wyoming graduate, who lives in the Wyoming town of Riverton with his wife, Jane, and children, Aimee, Adam, and Andrew.

Ms. Kent enjoys reading, music, theater, and travel. She loves to explore state and national parks and looks forward to spending more time in the Rocky Mountain states. She lives in Chicago with her husband, children's author R. Conrad Stein, and their daughter, Janna.

Photo Credits